A REALTOR'S
7
SECRETS OF
SUCCESS

JUSTIN M. BAKER

A Realtor's 7 Secrets of Success

©2023 Justin M. Baker

ISBN 979-8-35092-853-2
eBook ISBN 979-8-35092-854-9

CONTENTS

CHAPTER 1:

WHY NINETY PERCENT OF REALTORS FAIL?

To kick off our journey, we will delve into the various hurdles that realtors commonly come across during their inaugural year. These challenges serve as a defining factor that can determine their triumph or failure in the industry. Join me as we unravel these obstacles together and explore five crucial factors that play a pivotal role in their journey to success.

But wait, there's more! Not only will I reveal the top five reasons why realtors often face setbacks, but I have some exclusive bonus material prepared for you as well. Discover effective strategies and insights on how to overcome these obstacles and pave your way to a thriving real estate career.

The subsequent list is presented without a specific ranking order. Consequently, the reason assigned as number one does not necessarily denote the most prevalent cause for realtors' failure, and similarly, the reason labeled as number five does not necessarily signify the fifth most frequent factor.

- Poor team or brokerage selection: Making the wrong choice when selecting a brokerage or team can be a roadblock on the path to success.

- Lack of understanding of the role: Truly grasping the essence of being a realtor and gaining relevant experience is crucial.

- Inadequate financial preparation: Building a safety net of three to four months' worth of living expenses is essential to minimize stress.

- Self-management difficulties: Effective self-management skills are vital to overcoming setbacks and staying on track.

- Insufficient lead generation and follow-up: Generating enough leads and mastering follow-up skills are key ingredients for progress.

#1

One of the main reasons people often stumble in their endeavors is because they choose the wrong brokerage or team. This seemingly simple decision can have a significant impact. The brokerage landscape is a realm of endless possibilities: established giants with a rich fifty-year history or up-and-coming innovators. The choices for teams are just as abundant and diverse—it feels like you can find one on every corner. But here's the catch: most of these teams are plagued by . . .

Inefficiencies and suboptimal management.

In the vast realm of brokerages, it is paramount for individuals to exercise discernment and carefully evaluate their options. Picture established brokerages with decades of experience, who offer much more than stability and a proven track record. They possess a treasure trove of industry knowledge and a lasting presence, instilling unwavering confidence in those seeking reliability and unwavering trust.

On the flip side, emerging brokerages bring a breath of fresh air with their innovative approaches and new perspectives. These game-changers leverage cutting-edge technologies and strategies, propelling themselves to the forefront of industry advancements. If you're someone who thrives in an environment that embraces adaptability and welcomes change, these brokerages may just hold the golden ticket to your next exciting opportunity.

Beyond selecting a brokerage, lies a pivotal decision: the right team. With countless options out there, caution and due diligence are a must. Beware of teams plagued by inefficiency, ineffective leadership, and lack of unity. Joining a team isn't sufficient; seek one that exudes efficiency, synergy, and a shared vision—where success truly thrives.

By thoroughly analyzing the team's dynamics, structure, and communication channels, you can uncover a collaborative and supportive environment. It's in this nurturing space that individuals thrive, harnessing their strengths while benefiting from the collective expertise and guidance of their peers. The power of the right team acts as a catalyst, propelling individuals closer to their goals and multiplying their chances of achieving exceptional outcomes. Dare to dream big and watch the magic unfold!

Selecting the right brokerage and team is a game-changer. It's a decision that can either shape your professional journey towards triumph or pave a path to failure. With countless options at your fingertips, exercising prudence is key—weigh the pros and cons carefully. By aligning yourself with a reputable brokerage and a high-performing team, you'll supercharge your chances of success in your chosen endeavors. Choose wisely, and let greatness unfold!

#2

A second reason why realtors fail is two crucial aspects: a lack of understanding of the role and requirements of a realtor and a shortage of experience that hampers success in this field. So, how can you avoid falling into this challenging situation? It's time to break free from the misconceptions propagated by exaggerated portrayals of a realtor's life on TV. Instead, let's embark on a journey of discovery and understanding. Immerse yourself in thorough research to gain a comprehensive understanding of what a typical day in the life of a successful realtor truly entails. Engage proactively with accomplished realtors, seeking their valuable insights and inquiring about the insightful anecdotes and experiences that have shaped their professional journey. By immersing yourself in this wealth of knowledge, you equip yourself with the necessary tools and understanding to thrive in the real estate industry.

Once you have delved into some research, you will find a career as a realtor involves a multifaceted skill set required for success in this dynamic field. Many individuals, eager to obtain their license, often stumble due to a lack of understanding regarding the essential skills demanded by the profession. I've compiled a comprehensive list of skills that not only set apart a good realtor but are downright essential for thriving in the real estate world. From mastering finance and mortgage intricacies to honing sales and marketing prowess, from harnessing the power of social media to being a master of lead generation, these skills form the foundation of a real estate professional's toolkit. Beyond these, understanding CRM systems and effective follow-up, negotiating with finesse, navigating the legal landscape, and even having insights into construction and house-building processes can make a world of difference. Don't forget the critical aspects of title and escrow. Yet, amidst these tangible skills, it's equally vital to possess the intangible qualities of self-discipline and a relentless work ethic. In the pages ahead, we'll explore each of these skills in detail, providing you with the knowledge and tools to not only survive but thrive in the world of real estate.

#3

A third reason realtors often fail is because they're not financially prepared. They don't have enough savings to cover at least three to four months of living expenses. Let's talk about why having a financial cushion is so important and look into possible solutions to tackle this challenge.

The real estate profession is quite unique when it comes to income. Unlike typical salaried jobs where you can expect a regular paycheck, realtors often deal with fluctuating income that depends on successful transactions. So, it's unrealistic to expect a newly licensed realtor to sell their first home right away and get paid right after. In reality, it takes some time to establish yourself and build a client base.

Usually, it takes around a month or two for realtors to seal their first sale. But here's the catch—the payment doesn't come in right away. It can actually take another thirty to forty-five days for the deal to close and for the realtor to finally get their commission. So, you might end up going without a paycheck for a good three to four months. That's why having savings to cover your living expenses is crucial during this initial phase.

Now, let's talk solutions. One option is to save up a good amount of money before diving into the real estate industry. By setting aside funds to cover your living expenses for a few months, you'll have a financial buffer to help you through the early stages of your real estate career.

Another option is to consider having a part-time job while getting into real estate. By working part-time, you can make sure you have a steady income to cover your expenses while you're growing your real estate business. This approach gives you financial stability and takes away the pressure of having to make immediate real estate commissions.

On top of that, it can be really beneficial to join a real estate team that has a strong lead generation platform. Being part of a team gives you access to potential clients and listings, which can increase your chances of closing deals and earning commissions faster. Plus, when you leverage the team's established resources and clientele, you can really accelerate your income generation and minimize the time without a paycheck.

Having three to four months of living expenses saved is super important for realtors. The real estate income can be unpredictable, so having a financial safety net is a must to get through those first few months without earnings. Whether it's saving up in advance, working part-time, or teaming up with a successful real estate crew, aspiring realtors can tackle the financial challenges of starting their careers and set themselves up for long-term success in the industry.

#4

A fourth challenge that realtors often face is the difficulty in effectively managing themselves. Many realtors transition from previous jobs or careers where they had a manager or boss to organize their schedules, assign tasks, and hold them accountable. But when you become a realtor, you become an independent contractor and have the freedom to set your own schedule and manage your workload. This transition to self-management can be a big hurdle for many and can contribute to their failure in the industry.

The truth is, there's a good number of people who actually thrive when they have a boss telling them what to do and when to do it. They need that external accountability to stay focused and motivated. When they're left to manage themselves, things can get tough: prioritizing tasks becomes a challenge, time management goes haywire, and consistent productivity takes a hit. Without the structure and supervision they were used to in previous jobs, they often feel overwhelmed and struggle to stay disciplined enough to succeed.

Good news! Realtors have several options to tackle the challenge of self-management and boost their chances of success. One great strategy is to set up a schedule with time blocks for different tasks. By allocating dedicated time slots for activities like prospecting, client meetings, administrative work, and professional development, realtors can create a structured framework that increases productivity and ensures they consistently handle important responsibilities.

Joining a small accountability group within your brokerage or team can also be super beneficial. When you collaborate with like-minded peers who have similar goals and challenges, you create a supportive environment where you can hold each other accountable. Regular check-ins, sharing goals, and updating each other on progress within the group can really help you stay on track, maintain focus, and drive each other toward success.

Sharing and vocalizing one's goals with others can serve as an additional layer of accountability. By openly expressing their aspirations to colleagues, friends, or family members, realtors create a sense of responsibility and external pressure to follow through on their objectives. This added level of accountability can help individuals stay motivated, committed, and focused on achieving their goals.

If realtors find themselves struggling with self-management, hiring a real estate coach can be a game-changer. These professionals specialize in the real estate industry and can offer personalized guidance, mentorship, and accountability. They'll help you develop effective time management strategies, overcome self-discipline issues, and share invaluable insights for success in the industry. Make the investment and watch your business soar!

One of the biggest reasons why many realtors struggle is because of the challenge of self-management. But here's the thing—you can overcome this obstacle and thrive in your independent contractor role by implementing effective strategies. Yep, strategies like maintaining a schedule with time blocking, joining accountability groups, sharing goals with others, or even hiring a real estate coach. These steps will help you develop the self-discipline and structure you need to succeed!

#5

It is a common issue that many realtors, especially those who are new to the industry, struggle with efficient lead generation and effective follow-up strategies.

Entering into the realm of real estate can feel overwhelming and lead generation might be a completely new concept for newcomers. Understanding its significance is paramount as a lack of leads has the potential to be fatal for any business that relies on sales, real estate being no exception.

In this industry, the initial focus should be on what's referred to as the "check equity" type of lead generation. This involves leveraging various channels to get in front of potential clients and it's something every realtor should master.

Here are some options worth considering:

1. Marketing to your sphere of influence: This involves reaching out to the people you already know—family, friends, colleagues, and acquaintances, who might either be potential clients themselves or refer you to others.

2. Holding open houses: This can be an excellent way to meet potential clients face-to-face and showcase your skills in a real-world setting.

3. Door knocking: While it might sound old-school, this strategy involves personally reaching out to homeowners in targeted neighborhoods, which can be quite effective.

4. Cold calling For Sale by Owner (FSBO), expired, or canceled listings: This is a more direct approach where you reach out to homeowners who are trying to sell their property but are struggling. Offering your professional assistance could potentially turn these cold calls into hot leads.

5. Participating in networking events or groups: Joining local business networks, and real estate investment groups, or attending industry events can provide numerous opportunities to meet potential clients or referrals.

Furthermore, it's highly recommended to invest in a robust customer relationship management (CRM) system. This tool can help you track, nurture, and follow up with your leads systematically. A good CRM system can streamline your processes, reminding you when to reach out and keeping track of every interaction, ensuring no lead falls through the cracks. Effective lead generation coupled with efficient follow-up strategies can set you on the path to success in the real estate industry.

CHAPTER 2:

YOUR WHY REVEALS YOUR PASSION AND PURPOSE

The concept of "why" as explored in the text goes far beyond surface-level motivation. It delves into the core of who we are, pushing us to reflect on our purpose and seek meaningful fulfillment. Understanding our "why" becomes an anchor, guiding us through challenges and illuminating the path to a truly fulfilling life. Get ready to embark on a journey of self-discovery and unlock your greatest potential!

According to the brilliant Friedrich Nietzsche, "He who has a why can endure any how." This quote reminds us that our why, our deep-rooted purpose, becomes the driving force that empowers us to persevere in the face of adversity. When we have a clear sense of purpose and a strong reason behind our actions, we become unstoppable, conquering any obstacles that dare to challenge us on our journey.

Embarking on a journey of self-exploration and introspection, finding one's why becomes an exhilarating quest. It demands an honest examination of our strengths and weaknesses, unraveling the tapestry of our passions and values. As we delve deeper into these realms, our true selves emerge, and our purpose takes shape.

Discovering our why isn't just about professional success; it transcends all facets of life. It ignites a fire within us, guiding our decisions, fueling our ambitions, and granting us a sense of direction. When our actions align with our why, a symphony of fulfillment and purpose resonates through everything we do.

Beyond the realms of careers and industries, finding your why transforms your personal relationships and enriches your overall well-being. It becomes an unwavering anchor, offering solace amidst the storms and driving us forward in times of uncertainty.

The pursuit of your why is a perpetual odyssey of self-discovery and self-reflection. It means embracing your passions, comprehending your values, and forging an unwavering bond between your purpose and actions. By embracing your why, you unlock the gateways to a purposeful and gratifying existence. Stay true to your authentic self, and let your why become the driving force propelling you toward your aspirations.

"The two most important days in your life are the day you are born and the day you find out why."
—Mark Twain

Discovering Your Passion

Passion, the ultimate guidepost on the journey to discovering our "why," has the power to unlock success in both your real estate career and personal life. It ignites the fire of enthusiasm, fuels determination, and grants us a sense of purpose in everything we do.

Allow your interests and hobbies to be the launchpad that propels you toward your passions. Finding your passion is a unique and personal adventure, unveiling itself gradually, like a hidden treasure, over time. Don't be surprised if it catches you off guard, leading you to unexpected twists and turns in your career and personal pursuits. Embrace the excitement and fulfillment that comes with uncovering what truly drives your soul.

If you haven't found your passion yet, no need to worry! Let me share with you the inspiring journey of Colonel Sanders, the mastermind behind Kentucky Fried Chicken (KFC).

Born in 1890 in Indiana, USA, Sanders took on various jobs, from being a farmhand to a streetcar conductor and even an insurance salesman—but his true calling awaited. It wasn't until his mid-40s that Sanders discovered his love for cooking and crafted his legendary "secret recipe" for finger-lickin' good fried chicken.

At the remarkable age of sixty-two, in 1952, Sanders opened his first KFC restaurant in Salt Lake City, Utah, through franchising. Despite facing countless rejections along the way, Sanders remained persistent, and his unwavering determination led him to create a globally recognized brand beloved by many.

Colonel Sanders' late-in-life success story serves as a beacon of inspiration for all aspiring entrepreneurs, reminding us that it's never too late to pursue our passions and achieve incredible things. So keep exploring, stay hungry, and who knows? You might just discover something extraordinary!

Here's the twist: some folks stumble upon their passion at an impressively tender age. Take a look at Mozart, the musical maestro who left an indelible mark on classical composition. Born in 1756 in Salzburg, Austria, Mozart's prodigious talent in music became apparent from his earliest days.

At the mere age of three, Mozart masterfully played the keyboard and even began crafting his own melodies. By the time he reached five, he graced the presence of royals with his enchanting performances and captivating symphonies. Mozart's passion and innate aptitude for music were truly extraordinary, setting him on a mesmerizing journey that would span centuries.

Having multiple passions is not uncommon and can lead to remarkable combinations. Take Brian May, the renowned guitarist of Queen and astrophysicist. Yes, you read that right! His love for music and science coexist beautifully, showing us the power of pursuing diverse interests.

Now, let's dive deeper into the enchanting world of finding your passion. How can you find yours? Well, there are several clues waiting to be discovered. Pay close attention to your emotions, for they are your compass, guiding you toward activities that truly ignite your soul. Ask yourself, "What fills my heart with joy?" and "What sparks my curiosity, urging me to unravel its mysteries?" These questions hold the key to unlocking your passions.

Furthermore, pay heed to the skills that bring you joy and the activities that effortlessly capture your attention. These precious treasures will unveil even more hints on your path to finding your true passion. So, get ready to embark on this incredible journey of self-discovery!

Hobbies often serve as strong indicators of passion. Many individuals convert their hobbies into businesses or professional endeavors that they are truly passionate about. Unfortunately, some people may be aware of their passions but choose not to pursue them due to various reasons such as fear, societal expectations, or a lack of confidence.

An example of a famous person who turned their hobbies into a profession is Steve Jobs, the co-founder of Apple Inc. Steve Jobs was born in 1955 in San Francisco, California, and he developed a deep interest in electronics and technology from an early age.

In his early years, Jobs and his buddy Steve Wozniak shared an intense love for electronics. Together, they would tinker and build electronic gizmos in their humble garage. Little did they know that this playful pastime would soon spark the birth of Apple Computer Inc. in 1976. Their vision? To create user-friendly computers accessible to all.

But what began as a mere hobby transformed into an extraordinary journey for Steve Jobs. Apple, under his brilliant leadership, revolutionized the personal computer industry. And with groundbreaking products like the iPod, iPhone, and iPad, they left an indelible mark on the music, mobile, and tablet landscapes.

Jobs' extraordinary ability to channel his passion into a profession not only shaped his greatness but also revolutionized the world of technology and consumer electronics. His commitment to innovation and design continues to inspire countless entrepreneurs and creators to chase their dreams, transforming their passions into magnificent careers.

Passion serves as a compass on the journey to discovering your why. Exploring your interests, paying attention to your emotions, and recognizing the activities that bring you joy and fulfillment can help unveil your passions. Embracing your passions, whether they emerge early or later in life, can lead to a more purposeful and fulfilling path in both your professional and personal endeavors.

"Your time is limited, don't waste it living someone else's life. Don't be trapped by dogma, which is living the result of other people's thinking. Don't let the noise of other's opinion drown your own inner voice. And most important, have the courage to follow your heart and intuition, they somehow already know what you truly want to become." —Steve Jobs

---

Your Life's Purpose

Purpose serves as the foundation for our actions, thoughts, and behaviors. It is the driving force that propels us forward and gives meaning to our lives. Having a clear sense of purpose provides the motivation to wake up each morning with a sense of direction and the determination to make the most out of each day.

The connection between passion and purpose is significant. Your passion, which stems from your interests and desires, is channeled through your purpose in life. Purpose evolves and develops over time, shaped by new insights, experiences, and self-reflection. It is not a static concept, but rather a dynamic force that may require adjustments and realignments as you gain new perspectives.

Taking the time to step away from your daily routine and engage in reflection allows you to evaluate your purpose. Through introspection, you can assess whether your actions and choices align with your underlying values and aspirations. This process of re-evaluation and re-alignment helps you stay true to your authentic self and may involve stepping out of your comfort zone to explore new possibilities.

Purpose not only provides direction but also fuels a sense of fulfillment and increased motivation. When your actions are in line with your purpose, you experience a greater sense of satisfaction and find the drive to overcome obstacles and setbacks that come your way. Purpose enhances your decision-making abilities by providing a guiding framework that aligns with your values and long-term goals.

Setting goals and tracking progress through checklists can be game-changers. It's all about visualizing your efforts and holding yourself accountable. By measuring achievements, pinpointing areas for improvement, and staying focused, you'll be on fire to conquer your purpose! And, more on this later in the book.

And guess what? Surrounding yourself with like-minded individuals who share your values and aspirations adds even more fuel to your passion. They provide support, encouragement, and a sense of community that keeps spirits soaring high!

Remember, discovering your purpose is an ongoing journey, not an instant revelation. It's about exploring within, reflecting on yourself, and having the flexibility to adapt and evolve while gaining new experiences and insights. Your purpose is personal, unique, and a reflection of your values, passions, and aspirations. Embrace it!

Purpose serves as a driving force that gives direction and meaning to our lives. It is an evolving concept that requires self-reflection and realignment as we gain new insights and experiences. Discovering and embracing our purpose leads to a greater sense of fulfillment, motivation, and resilience, allowing us to make decisions in alignment with our values and long-term goals. By setting goals, tracking progress, and surrounding ourselves with like-minded individuals, we can nurture our purpose and strive for a more purposeful and rewarding life journey.

Engaging in hobbies can provide valuable insights into your passions, and many individuals transform their hobbies into fulfilling businesses with purpose. Regrettably, there are individuals who acknowledge their genuine passion yet fall short in its pursuit. They never unlock the potential of blending passion with purpose, missing out on a remarkable synergy that awaits.

Discovering your genuine passion is an exhilarating journey, and fortunately, there's a powerful and transformative system to expertly guide you along the way. Brace yourself for a life-changing experience as this meticulously crafted system unravels the hidden depths of your true passions. Get ready to step into a world filled with purpose and fulfillment like never before! Embrace the opportunity to explore your unique interests and unleash your full potential with this extraordinary system—the Ikigai framework.

Imagine a Japanese concept called Ikigai that translates to "reason for being" or "purpose in life." It's a holistic approach that goes beyond finding what you love. It aligns your passions, skills, values, and the needs of the world, enchanting you with a life of meaning and fulfillment.

"Your purpose in life is to find your purpose and give your whole heart and soul to it."
—Gautama Buddha

Ready to dive in? Let's explore the four overlapping elements of the Ikigai framework:

1. Passion: What sets your soul on fire? What activities bring you unbridled joy and fulfillment, making your heart race with excitement?

2. Skills: What are your secret weapons? Reflect on your strengths and areas of expertise. Identify the skills you possess or can develop further on your journey to fulfillment.

3. Values: What truly matters to you? Dig deep into your core beliefs and principles. Discover your deepest convictions and consider the impact you aspire to make in the world.

4. Market Demand: How can you contribute? What pressing problems or needs can you address? Identify ways to create value for others and make a positive difference in the world.

By weaving together these four elements, you'll uncover the intricate tapestry of your genuine passion and purpose. Discover the sweet spot where your passion harmonizes with your skills, values, and the needs of the world. Step into a life of balance, fulfillment, and profound meaning.

Are you ready to embark on this extraordinary journey? Let the Ikigai framework be your guiding light!

It's important to note that the Ikigai framework is a personal journey, and it requires self-reflection, exploration, and experimentation. It may involve trying new experiences, seeking feedback, and adapting along the way. Ultimately, the goal is to find that sweet spot where your passion, skills, values, and the world's needs converge, leading you to a fulfilling and purposeful life.

It is crucial to select a passion in which you can genuinely succeed. Guessing or setting unrealistic aspirations will only lead to inevitable failure. Secondly, your chosen passion should align with your mental and physical capabilities, ensuring that it is within reach. Thirdly, it is essential for your passion to be specific, as pursuing vague or undefined interests can result in wasted time and effort. Additionally, you must establish a means of measuring your progress to determine if your chosen passion is the right fit for you. Evaluating the advancements or setbacks you experience can provide valuable insights into the suitability of your chosen path. It is important to consider if your passion aligns with a feasible action plan when embarking on the journey to discover your true purpose in life.

"The meaning of life is to find your gift. The purpose of life is to give it away." —Pablo Picasso

---

Connecting Purpose with Passion

Passion extends far beyond a mere interest or hobby. While an interest or hobby may captivate our attention for a while, passion goes deeper, igniting a fire within us that compels us to take action and pursue our dreams. Connecting our passion with our purpose creates a powerful alliance that can have transformative effects throughout our lives. Purpose is a deep conviction, a driving force that gives meaning and direction to our actions, while passion fuels our emotions and brings joy and enthusiasm to what we do. When these two elements align, they set us on a path toward a fulfilling life.

When passion and purpose are not related or in sync, a sense of fulfillment and satisfaction becomes elusive. Without a clear connection between our passions and our purpose, we can easily fall into burnout and feel a sense of emptiness in our endeavors. It is crucial to identify the interplay between our passions and purpose to experience a truly meaningful and rewarding life.

Sometimes, as we reflect on our lives, we stumble upon an epiphany—our passion has always resided within us, patiently waiting to be acknowledged and nurtured. This revelation brings an incredible surge of clarity and purpose, propelling us toward a life of meaning and fulfillment.

Yet, there are those who find themselves adrift in a sea of uncertainty, their passion and purpose disjointed. They wander through diverse interests and occupations, lacking a compass to find their true path or understand their authentic selves. It's akin to venturing into a dense jungle without a discernible way forward.

However, I firmly believe that each and every one of us holds the potential to uncover our passion and purpose, or even cultivate a purpose that blossoms into a fiery passion. The search for these vital elements can be facilitated through introspection and the guiding hand of a mentor or coach, adding enlightening insights and valuable direction to our quest.

Discovering your why is a journey that will truly captivate you. Reflect on the tapestry of your life, exploring the activities that touch lives and those that make time fly. Delve into your childhood, reminiscing your happiest moments and the pure joy they brought. Picture doing something effortlessly, not even needing to be paid for it. It's through uncovering your passion and watching it bloom into purpose that you unlock the daily joy and fulfillment that make work rewarding and exhilarating.

When your why, purpose, and passion align, you become boundless, invincible even. Imagine yourself standing on a narrow plank between towering buildings, buffeted by a wild wind. Without a strong reason, you might hesitate and decline. But suppose the safety of your loved ones depended on your actions. Suddenly, your response would be a resolute and emphatic "yes!" With your purpose, passion, and why at the forefront, you would muster the courage and strength to overcome any obstacle that dare cross your path.

Contemplating Friedrich Nietzsche's timeless quote, "He who has a why can endure any how." We rediscover its unwavering truth. Nevertheless, our modern world offers us an array of additional resources and tools to navigate our life's journey. Engaging the aid of a professional coach, for instance, can smoothen our path, bestowing us with guidance, revelations, and accountability. Consequently, we unravel a more captivating and gratifying existence. In essence, the nexus of passion and purpose is a transformative voyage that infuses our lives with significance, guidance, and contentment. It necessitates introspection, self-reflection, and aligning our pursuits with our principles and aspirations. When our passions harmonize with our purpose, obstacles dissipate, and our daily endeavors brim with elation, transforming our lives into a compelling narrative driven by a profound sense of purpose.

"Your work is going to fill a large part of your life, and the only way to be truly satisfied is to do what you believe is great work. And the only way to do great work is to love what you do."—Steve Jobs

---

AROUND THE BLOCK...
INTERVIEWS WITH TOP ECHELON REAL ESTATE
PROFESSIONALS ABOUT THEIR WHY...

Carin Nguyen,

The Carin Nguyen Real Estate Network, Phoenix, Arizona

A significant portion of my journey traces back to my childhood experiences. As soon as I reached the eligible age of around fifteen and ten months, or a little before I turned sixteen legally, I obtained my first job. At the age of nineteen, I even purchased a house. The primary drive behind my actions during that time was to establish a certain level of security in my life. It all ties back to Maslow's hierarchy of needs, where my fundamental human necessities were being met.

Growing up, I had to cope with considerable instability and a lack of security. I attended a total of thirteen different schools and moved frequently. When you experience such frequent changes and transitions, it becomes apparent that you are now responsible for your well-being and providing for yourself.

Once I achieved a level of stability and security for myself and my family, my focus shifted toward teaching others. This is the phase I find myself in today. I contemplate how I can help others attain the same lifestyle and use their businesses to fund the life they genuinely desire.

I came to realize that when you concentrate on what you don't want, you tend to attract exactly that because your brain struggles to negate the concept of "don't." It took me some time, perhaps as recent as six or seven years ago, to break free from that cycle. At that point, my focus shifted authentically toward assisting others. However, I firmly believe that before you can genuinely care for and help others, you must ensure that your own needs are met. Once I acknowledged that I had taken care of myself, I was able to channel my energy toward supporting and teaching others.

The why behind my desire to teach others and help them navigate their journeys emerged around seven years ago. It became a true passion, fueled by the understanding that I had the ability to guide and empower individuals to create the life they desire.

My early experiences and the need for security led me to focus on providing for myself. Eventually, I reached a point where my own needs were met, allowing me to shift my attention to assisting others. This transition occurred about seven years ago, marking the beginning of my authentic passion for teaching and supporting others on their paths to success.

Daniel Beer,
Daniel Beer Home Team CEO & Owner, San Diego, California

In earlier years, my focus was centered around proving myself and answering questions like, "Will I succeed? Will I be able to provide for my family? Can I surpass the accomplishments of my predecessors?" There was a constant need to understand my worth and intelligence.

Over time, my why has evolved. Initially, I believed that I needed to do more and provide beyond what was given to me. It's not a complaint; I received a lot. However, I felt that true growth lay in the ability to enhance and improve upon what was already there. It became a personal challenge to see how I could elevate my circumstances.

When I encounter tough days or face challenges now, I recognize that it is ultimately my responsibility. I am the one who has the power to determine how I respond and whether or not I allow it to impact me negatively. Taking ownership of my experiences allows me to navigate through tough times without letting them define my entire day.

At this point in my journey, what truly drives me is the sheer enjoyment of it all. I find pleasure in the process, in striving to win, and in the financial rewards that come with success. The combination of these elements fuels my motivation and keeps me moving forward.

My earlier years were driven by a need to prove myself and exceed expectations. However, my why has transformed into a pursuit of personal enjoyment, the thrill of winning, and the satisfaction of financial growth.

Katharine Loucaidou
Real Estate Group, Bolton, Ontario

The driving force behind my decision to enter the real estate industry was a strong desire to pursue something different from teaching. I had reached a point where I unequivocally declared to myself that I never wanted to teach again. It was a phase of seeking a second chance at life, a fresh start. As I ventured into real estate, I soon realized the immense potential I had to help people.

Witnessing the positive impact I could make in the lives of others through real estate was a revelation. The more I immersed myself in the field, expanding my knowledge and expertise, the more effectively I could assist people in navigating through potentially problematic situations. This realization transformed my why into a question: How can I educate and guide individuals to put them on the right path?

Not everyone possesses a clear understanding of what they truly want or how to achieve it. I found fulfillment in supporting others in discovering their aspirations and helping them align their actions accordingly. This became a significant aspect of my why—to assist people in finding their direction and purpose within the real estate realm.

As I continued to gain experience and pursued higher levels of education in the industry, such as obtaining my broker's license, my why further evolved. I began to contemplate the possibility of transferring the wealth of knowledge I had acquired to other agents. This led me to envision opening a brokerage that would challenge the traditional norms. I aspired to create an anti-brokerage, where individuals were not treated as mere numbers but rather as valued professionals.

My aim was to have a genuine impact and demonstrate to agents that professionalism can thrive within the industry. I aimed to break away from the stereotype of the "used car salesman" image by emphasizing the importance of learning proper communication methods and showing genuine care for clients. I believed that by instilling these values, agents could elevate their businesses and reshape the perception of the industry.

My initial motivation for entering real estate was a desire for a fresh start away from teaching. However, as I witnessed the positive impact I could make in people's lives, my why shifted toward educating and guiding individuals to find their path within the real estate realm. With further experience and education, I aimed to share my knowledge with other agents and challenge industry norms by fostering professionalism and genuine care for clients.

Randy Byrd,
Broker, eXp Reality, Santa Rosa, California

My driving force, my why, has always been inspired by Zig Ziglar's philosophy: "Helping others get what they want will ultimately help you get what you want." This aligns perfectly with my natural inclination to assist and support others. It brings me immense satisfaction and fulfillment.

As I have grown and expanded my reach, I have discovered a deep passion for helping people who may never be able to repay me or even realize that I am assisting them. There is a profound sense of power in making a positive impact on others' lives without any expectation of recognition or reciprocation.

Coaching, training, mentoring, and engaging in success coaching are all facets of my why. These activities allow me to have a significant influence on others, guiding them to discover their own why and what they truly desire in life. When individuals connect with their passions and understand the impact they can have on themselves, their families, and the world at large, they become unstoppable. It empowers them to rise above the trivialities and challenges of everyday life.

Throughout my journey, I have acquired valuable knowledge and experiences. I attribute my realization of the importance of helping others to my time working with Tom Ferry as a coach, and even earlier during my tenure as a team leader and trainer at Keller Williams. Tom Ferry, in particular, played a crucial role in bringing out this aspect of my why. I cherished the coaching relationship we had, and I am grateful for his contributions to my growth. While I have since evolved and moved beyond that phase, I have no regrets. I treasure the moments I spent with my coaches, like yourself and Bill Pipes, as they have transformed me into the person I am today and continue to shape my future.

Bic DeCaro

and Associates, eXp Realty, Ashburn Virginia

When I initially entered the business, it was through the recruitment of my brother. At that time, I didn't have a clear why or purpose other than wanting to fulfill myself and find personal satisfaction.

Being immersed in the retail world, I was accustomed to working long hours and dedicating my efforts to someone else's business. However, I began to realize the potential of redirecting that same level of dedication and hard work toward building my own business. It sparked the idea that by thinking more like a leader, I could not only achieve personal growth but also have the opportunity to lead and assist others. Initially, I didn't see those leadership qualities within myself. I viewed myself more as a worker bee, simply executing tasks without recognizing my potential for leadership.

My initial why stemmed from the desire to create stability for my future family. I wanted to avoid the constant upheaval of moving from place to place, providing a sense of security and consistency for my loved ones. Simultaneously, I discovered a genuine passion for helping people. This passion gradually became a central aspect of my why, motivating me to make a positive impact in the lives of others.

In summary, when I started in the business, my primary motivation was the desire for personal fulfillment. However, as I began to realize the potential for personal and professional growth, coupled with a desire to create stability for my future family, my why evolved. Helping others became a significant driver, fueling my passion and shaping my purpose in the business.

Lindsay Stevens,
eXp Reality, Hudson Valley, New York

Over the years, my why has undergone a transformation. Initially, when I entered the real estate industry, my primary motivation was to create a bright and beautiful life for my family and children. However, as I progressed in my journey, I evolved into a leader.

Now, my why is centered around using real estate as a powerful vehicle to help others achieve their dreams, hopes, and desires. This mission is ingrained in the team I am a part of, and it is well-known to everyone involved. We are a group of like-minded professionals who are fiercely committed to raising the standards and pushing the boundaries in the real estate industry.

Together, as a team, we are dedicated to elevating the industry locally. We strive to support and challenge each other, pushing ourselves beyond our comfort zones to accomplish personal and professional growth. Real estate serves as the means to achieve these goals. We believe that by nurturing our professional growth, we can fund and achieve everything we aspire to in our personal lives.

In summary, my why has shifted from creating a better life for my family to using real estate as a vehicle to enable others to achieve their dreams. As part of a dedicated team, we are committed to raising the bar in the industry and pushing ourselves to reach new heights personally and professionally. The growth we experience in our real estate endeavors fuels the fulfillment of our personal aspirations.

Larry White,

eXp Reality, Houston, Texas

For me, this is something I speak about in almost every group of agents that I talk to, because if you don't have the why, it's hard to keep going when life gets in the way. I actually share my why with people and it's $4.38. Early in my career, I made a lot of money and thought I was done with life and had it all figured out until I lost even more. And so my why comes from the money, being down, and stuff that wasn't really the issue.

I had met my bride in our senior year at Arizona State and she was the one. She was always the one that got away. We had the most explosive six months. But we were both Libras, really laissez-faire. So we were okay; we didn't want to do long distance. So if we were both single when we came back, we would continue dating. Every six months I would call and say, "Hey do you want to go to Costa Rica?"

She said, "I have a boyfriend."

I said, "Is that a yes? Is that a no?"

Finally, eight years later, I invited her to do this non-profit with me. It was called Shoe for Africa. We would collect used running shoes at PF Chang's Rock and Roll Marathon. Then we would ship them to a counterpart in Kenya and they would pass them out to villages because a lot of people were walking around barefoot.

And so I called her. She was like, "Well, yeah let's go."

I said, "Let's go grab a coffee and talk about it." And my card was declined for $4.38. It was one of the low points, the pain, the shame, the embarrassment. I felt it because this was the woman of my dreams at this point in time. And so that was my leverage. And now I compounded it. We were not in that situation anymore.

But what if I was paying for my kids' birthday party and my card was declined? And now I pass on that shame and that embarrassment. So, for me, it has to be bigger than you because most people are, well, I'll get by not eating. I tell people it's almost like the rule of seven.

I ask so many agents and the most common answer is what do you want to do? The most common answer is "I want to make a hundred thousand dollars."

I say, "Why, because the difference between sixty and a hundred thousand dollars is not changing your life unless you set that extra $40,000 up."

And then they'll say, "Well, you know that will allow me to pay all my bills." Okay, well why is that important? And then they'll say, "I view that as somebody who is successful." Why do you view that person is important and I keep digging down seven different levels. Now you'll start to get to the reality of what's going to drive you. That's three levels of why imagine continuing to deal down.

That's the leverage that you need to have to get you through, "Oh I don't feel good; I don't want to make my calls today."

CHAPTER 3:

ARE YOU COACHABLE?

Embracing change is no easy feat—it's an unavoidable part of life's roller coaster ride. But fear not, for there's a beacon of hope amidst the chaos: a wise soul who's weathered life's storms and helped others navigate their own seas of change. Enter the role of being coachable. Ah, the beauty of possessing a mindset open to growth, ready to sail uncharted territories with a trusted guide.

Now, when it comes to hiring a coach, remember, they don't have to be a master of your craft or have walked in your exact shoes. Take Michael Jordan and Tiger Woods, for instance. These legends had coaches who may not have possessed their extraordinary skills, but they understood the principles of success like no other.

Sure, experience counts, but don't underestimate the power of a coach who's an avid student of your craft. Sometimes, their deep understanding and remarkable expertise in your specific domain can unlock hidden insights and propel you to new heights. So set sail on the voyage to greatness, with a coach by your side, as you conquer the ever-changing tides of life.

When it comes to finding success in the dynamic real estate industry, having the guidance of an experienced real estate coach can be a game-changer. Coaching becomes not just a process, but a vital ally that you willingly embrace, agree with, and actively seek out. You're at the helm of carefully selecting a coach, interviewing potential candidates, and thoroughly assessing their backgrounds. While it's tempting to let someone's personality sway you, remember to prioritize performance over personality. Finding the perfect coach requires a comprehensive understanding of their expertise and alignment with your goals.

But that's just the beginning. Once you find that ideal coach, it's all about commitment. Genuine dedication to the coaching process is what sets you on the path to success. Without it, you risk wasting your time, the coach's time, and your financial investment. So, approach coaching with unwavering determination and a willingness to actively participate in the process. Get ready to unlock your true potential and soar to new heights!

The path to change becomes smoother with the guidance of a coach. Being coachable means embracing support, regardless of your coach's expertise. In the ever-evolving real estate industry, an experienced real estate coach offers valuable insights and guidance. However, finding the right coach calls for thoughtful consideration of their background and an unwavering commitment to the coaching process for remarkable results. Let the journey begin!

"Stay hungry, stay humble. Always be teachable. Always be a student." —Will Smith

---

Coachable Criteria

Are you coachable? It's a question that requires introspection—an inward examination of your mindset, your curiosity, your willingness to learn, your accountability, and your humility. Knowing where you stand in life and your career is crucial for progress. By understanding your current circumstances, you can pave the way for your future aspirations. It's through self-awareness that you define your goals and shape the person you want to become.

But being coachable is more than just possessing certain traits. It's about committing to behavioral changes that drive improved outcomes in sales, leadership, and life. Coachable individuals understand that there's always room for growth. They embrace alternative methods and approaches to elevate both their personal and professional endeavors, including real estate.

So ask yourself, are you ready to be coachable?

If you're convinced that you're always right and have an inflated ego, I'm going to pause you right there. Take a breather and put the brakes on, because ego can be a real roadblock to growth and progress in coaching. But don't worry, we'll tackle this issue head-on in the next chapter!

Coaching is an incredible journey of self-discovery, where we'll dive deep into your personality and embrace change. And let's be honest, change is tough, but it's the key to unlocking personal growth. The time it takes to form new habits varies for everyone, from a mere twenty-one days to a whole year. It all depends on your ability to ditch the detrimental habits, adopt positive approaches, and how quickly you blaze your own trail to personal development. So, let's get started, shall we?

Unlocking your coachability requires more than just following a checklist. It's about embracing the challenges, conquering the barriers, and igniting a burning desire for growth. How? By actively listening, probing with insightful questions, and fearlessly acting on feedback. Set those crystal-clear goals, track your progress, and refuse to settle for average.

Coachability is a journey, and it starts with evaluating yourself honestly. Leave no stone unturned, no comfort zones unchallenged. Overcome resistance, break free from fear, and shed that defensive armor. Embrace change as your ally, paving the way for personal and professional greatness.

In this adventure, strategic tools like active listening and goal setting become your compass, steering you toward the realm of unlimited progress. Cultivate a mindset that is hungry for coaching, and watch your success grow exponentially at every step. Ready to embark on this coaching odyssey?

Personality and Introspection

Personality is like a canvas of colors, blending feelings, thoughts, and behaviors unique to each one of us. It's what makes us who we are, evolving and growing with time.

Imagine having a skilled coach who not only understands and values your uniqueness but also helps you harness your strengths. They can even unlock the secrets of navigating different personality types, empowering you to have more meaningful interactions.

Intrigued? Many coaches recommend personality tests that offer detailed insights into your inner workings. Trust me, these tests are not just intriguing, they're downright illuminating!

Introspection is a powerful journey of self-reflection, where we delve deep into our inner thoughts and emotions. It's a process that requires setting aside our ego and the constant urge to be right. During introspection, we embrace positive and empowering language, helping us and our coach gain profound insights into our current position. We uncover the factors that have either propelled or hindered our progress in the past.

Sometimes, we find ourselves stuck, encountering challenges that feel like failures and leave us disheartened. But fret not, for these moments are merely opportunities in disguise. That's where a coach comes in—a catalyst for the change we seek. They guide us toward solutions, empowering us to overcome obstacles and unleash our true potential. Let introspection be your compass on this transformative journey, leading you to incredible growth.

When diving into introspection, it's crucial to envision the ultimate recipe for success and happiness. Reflect on thought-provoking queries like "What does success truly mean to me?" and "What brings me genuine happiness?" These soul-searching explorations will provide clarity, forging a path for your personal and professional odyssey.

Want to make introspection more rewarding? Seek the guidance of a seasoned real estate coach. Many folks struggle to embark on this solitary journey without proper support or patience. Remember, uncovering your past, evaluating the present, and shaping your desired future all hinge on candid introspection. Get ready to embark on a transformative quest!

Personality is a captivating blend of inherent and acquired traits that make you wonderfully unique. Embrace introspection, a powerful tool for self-reflection and growth, paving the way to your success and happiness. And along this enlightening journey, seek the guidance and support of an experienced real estate coach to elevate your introspective process to new heights.

The Art of Being Coachable

To establish a thriving coaching relationship, it's vital to grasp the roles of both the coach and yourself, cultivating a connection built on trust and accountability. This journey demands an open mind, a hunger for knowledge, an insatiable curiosity, and a touch of humility.

The coach's mission is to help you conquer the barriers hindering your performance and introduce transformative concepts for growth. Moreover, a coach can guide you in exploring new horizons and unearthing hidden opportunities. But remember the true power lies in your coachability. When you find yourself stuck, don't hesitate to seek guidance and support—it might just be the catalyst you need to unlock an extraordinary life.

"The greatest teacher is the one who says, 'You can do it,' and then helps you to discover what you can do on your own." —Lou Holtz

Embrace the art of being coachable: a key ingredient in unlocking your professional and personal potential. It calls for an open mind, a willingness to receive guidance, and the ability to follow instructions.

Unearth growth within the discomfort, and let failure be your greatest teacher. Even success holds secrets about your inner self. Embrace failures, extract priceless wisdom, and unlock a future brimming with boundless opportunities. Reach new heights, powered by the discomfort that leads to genuine progress.

When partnering with a coach, be prepared for their keen eye to catch common mistakes or flawed processes. It's natural to feel defensive when your work or methods are critiqued, but it's crucial to overcome that instinct. Remind yourself that the coach's goal is your improvement and greater success. Embrace this opportunity for growth by letting go of defensiveness, opening your mind, and wholeheartedly committing to making necessary changes. Remember, a coach isn't just a friend. They're here to challenge you and push you to unlock your full potential in life and business.

Remember, your coach genuinely cares about your growth and has your best interests at heart when offering feedback. It's natural to feel uncertain at first, as change can be challenging. But embracing a transformative journey takes dedication and perseverance. There may be bumps along the road, but with unwavering determination, you'll pave the way to exciting and addictive triumphs. So, let's make a habit of pushing harder and let the thrill of success ignite our passion!

Creating a successful coaching relationship is a thrilling journey! It's about grasping the roles of the coach and yourself, building a strong connection, and embracing accountability. To be coachable, you need an open mind, a thirst for learning, curiosity, and humility. Remember, discomfort and failure pave the way for growth—they're the stepping stones to success! Be receptive to feedback, conquer defensiveness, and be ready to make changes. Your coach is your ally, challenging and supporting you towards improvement, always with your best interests at heart. So, let's dive into the thrilling journey of change and savor the addictive rewards of success!

"A coach is someone who can give correction without causing resentment."—John Wooden

---

Those Not Ready for the Coaching Experience

Embarking on the journey of personal and professional growth requires conquering obstacles head-on. Addressing common hurdles like the fear of failure, resistance to change, defensive behavior, and self-awareness gaps is key. Don't let these flaws deter your coaching experience and career. The good news? They're totally fixable! Embrace them, become self-aware, and take actionable steps toward improvement. You've got this!

1. Prepare yourself for countless rejections, for it is through these obstacles that triumph is achieved!

Let's consider these behaviors honestly:

1. Negative attitude: Persistence, my friend, is the magic key that unlocks success. In the world of sales, a negative attitude is like a dead-end street. Prepare yourself for countless rejections, for it is through these obstacles that triumph is achieved!

2. Defensiveness: Don't let defensiveness hinder your ability to see things from different angles. Whether you're in a coaching relationship or sales, being open to feedback is absolutely crucial. Let that growth mindset lead the way!

3. Lack of feedback-seeking: If you hesitate to seek feedback from others about your ideas, it's time to embrace vulnerability and open yourself up to a world of insights and perspectives. Let the power of collaboration and diverse viewpoints shape your journey toward growth and success.

4. Resistance to change: Change is a constant force, propelling us toward success. In the rapid whirlwind of today's business world, the ability to adapt becomes a powerful asset.

5. Poor listening skills: Effective communication is all about active listening. Just remember, you've got two ears and one mouth for a reason! So, take a moment, slow down, and really tune in to what others have to say. You never know what valuable insights and knowledge you might gain.

6. Reluctance to ask for help: Independence is truly admirable, but let's not forget the immense value woven within seeking assistance. Asking for help is not a sign of weakness, but rather a golden opportunity for personal growth and continuous learning. Embrace it!

7. Disregard for constructive criticism: Embracing constructive criticism is a gateway to personal and professional growth. By actively listening to others and valuing their insights, we unlock the potential for collaborative development and progress. Embrace the power of shared knowledge and fuel your journey toward success!

8. Avoidance of challenges: Challenges may seem daunting at first, but hidden within them lie boundless opportunities for growth and success. So, let's wholeheartedly embrace these challenges, actively seek out solutions, and cultivate an unwavering mindset of resilience. You can conquer anything that comes your way!

9. Victim mentality: Stop blaming others and feeling sorry for yourself! It's counterproductive. Take charge and own your actions and choices. Empower yourself to make positive change happen!

10. Dismissing others' ideas: Don't let stubbornly clinging to your ideas be a barrier to growth. Embrace the power of open-mindedness, exploring alternative solutions, and valuing the contributions of others. You can achieve beyond your wildest imagination!

11. Failure to recognize others' contributions: Recognizing and appreciating the incredible positive contributions of others is an absolute game-changer, both in your career and in life. It's all about teamwork, and when you wholeheartedly acknowledge the immense value others bring, you pave the way for even greater achievements. Celebrate the power of collaboration!

Unlock the full potential of your coaching journey by proactively tackling these obstacles. Discover a more fulfilling career that blooms with personal growth. Embrace change, feedback, and collaboration—the keys to unlocking greatness!

"A coach is someone who tells you what you don't want to hear, who has you see what you don't want to see, so you can be who you have always known you could be." —Tom Landry

---

The Coaching Process and Results

To cultivate coachability, embrace strategies like active listening, curious questioning, embracing feedback, acting upon it, setting goals, and monitoring progress. These practices pave the way for your growth and triumph in the coaching journey.

A successful coaching experience thrives on effective and candid communication. Unlock the power of open dialogue for a deeper understanding and invaluable guidance. Transparency and openness lay a solid groundwork for progress and remarkable achievements. Let's embark on this transformative partnership!

Get ready to level up in the coaching process! Expect unbiased constructive criticism and fresh perspectives that shed light on areas for improvement. Your coach will be your rock, holding you accountable as you crush your attainable goals. Remember, the discomfort of accountability is just a stepping stone towards personal and professional growth!

Discover the power of a coach! They'll be your guide, helping you shape and organize your business. Identify areas for improvement and highlight your strengths.

To make the most of this coaching relationship, honesty and transparency are key! Share your goals, finances, systems, and team with them. Together, you'll conquer new heights!

Step into the coaching zone with an open mind and leave your ego behind. Embrace the coach's guidance and ditch the excuses that hold you back. It's time to make positive changes and align your actions with your goals.

In the coaching relationship, authenticity is everything. Don't pretend to agree just to avoid criticism. Instead, be open and transparent, treating your coach like a trusted confidant. Share your thoughts and concerns honestly, just as you would with a trusted psychiatrist. You'll unlock your true potential!

With coaching, your self-confidence soars, empowering you to conquer short and long-term goals. Experience the pinnacle of real estate success and personal happiness. Coaching offers priceless professional guidance, far superior to navigating the journey alone. Remember, everyone needs a coach, but being coachable is equally vital. You will amplify your potential!

"Success doesn't come easy," as Vince Lombardi, the legendary football coach, once said. It takes dedication and effort. When you say yes to coaching, you commit to putting in the work required for success. Embrace this opportunity to push yourself harder, think smarter, and give that extra effort; knowing it will contribute to the triumph of your coaching journey.

Recognize the immense benefits of being coachable. It fosters continuous growth and the development of your coaching skills. Embrace the exhilarating journey of growth and development, always knowing your coach stands by your side, supporting you every step of the way.

The Group Coaching Alternative

Joining a real estate coaching group with multiple participants can do wonders for your growth. Imagine the benefits of connecting with like-minded individuals who share your interests and goals. Together, we form a supportive community where we can freely exchange ideas, celebrate successes, tackle challenges, and learn from personal experiences. This collective wisdom and shared knowledge fuel our understanding and propel us forward.

Habits are hard to change, but within our group, the process becomes more manageable. We hold each other accountable, supporting one another in breaking unproductive patterns and developing new, positive ones. Together, we create a sense of responsibility and motivation that drives personal and professional growth.

But it goes beyond that—the power of relating to others is immense. When we find common ground with our leader, mentor, coach, or fellow group members, change becomes natural. We become a tight-knit community, empowering and reinforcing each other's new behaviors. It's like the positive impact of gym classes, CrossFit, or church communities.

Within our group, there is no shortage of advice, encouragement, and creative solutions. Our diverse perspectives and experiences create a collective reservoir of knowledge and innovative thinking. Think of the possibilities!

Each week, our group meetings give our coach a chance to evaluate our progress, provide tailored guidance, and offer constructive criticism. You'll receive individualized attention, fine-tuning your strategies and keeping you laser-focused on your objectives.

And let's not forget about the networking opportunities. Our group setting is a hub of connections and collaborations. Need client referrals? Financing information? Insights into local real estate laws? Our community has your back. It's a fertile ground for expanding your professional horizons.

Being part of this coaching group instills the importance of coachability and nurtures continual skill development. The support and encouragement from fellow group members act as a catalyst for personal and professional advancement.

In a nutshell, joining this real estate coaching group with multiple participants is your dynamic platform for learning, support, accountability, and networking. It fosters a sense of community and equips you with the resources needed to achieve both individual and collective success. So, what are you waiting for?

"Great coaches help you see the invisible, hear the unsaid, and believe the incredible." —Unknown

---

AROUND THE BLOCK...
INTERVIEWS WITH TOP ECHELON REAL ESTATE PROFESSIONALS, REGARDING BEING COACHABLE.

Carin Nguyen,
The Carin Nguyen Real Estate Network, Phoenix, Arizona

The key to being coachable lies in your willingness to receive feedback and take action based on that feedback. It is closely connected to being responsible, which means taking ownership of your circumstances instead of playing the victim. Rather than attributing everything to external factors or others, ask yourself, "How did I contribute to this situation?" Even in situations like a car accident where you are not at fault, acknowledging your responsibility in being present at that moment is important. Remember, it was an accident caused by another driver.

Taking ultimate responsibility in every situation aligns with being coachable. It goes beyond simply accepting feedback; it involves being accountable and actively seeking ways to make changes and grow.

Personally, I have multiple coaches in different areas. For personal development, mindset, and energy perspectives. Having different coaches allows me to benefit from their expertise and guidance in specific areas.

Daniel Beer,
Daniel Beer Home Team CEO & Owner, San Diego, California

The essence of it is quite straightforward. It revolves around whether someone executes the plan as it was designed or if they feel the need to make adjustments. It's about having faith in the plan versus overthinking it. Ultimately, it boils down to taking action and following through.

My coach supports me in various aspects. He plays a role in helping us enhance our recruitment and retention strategies, as well as our overall organizational structure. However, what has pleasantly surprised me is that he has also been instrumental in my personal development journey.

Through his coaching, I have grown in my leadership skills and learned to take ownership of my power instead of relinquishing it to others. This shift in self-responsibility has had a significant impact on many aspects of my life.

My coach guides me on how to effectively lead, especially during challenging conversations and uncomfortable situations He teaches me to confront issues directly to prevent them from escalating into drama. His coaching focuses on leading based on standards rather than personal preferences, which simplifies life tremendously. Additionally, he provides guidance on nutrition, physical fitness, and personal appearance, encompassing a holistic approach to development.

Katharine Loucaidou,
Real Estate Group, Bolton, Ontario

Currently, my coaches are individuals in industries that have a profound impact. I observe and learn from them, incorporating some of their practices into my own. I make it a point to listen to podcasts and read extensively, constantly seeking new ideas and perspectives.

At the moment, I'm immersed in Tony Robbins' book, and I believe that being coachable entails not only listening to valuable ideas but also taking action to implement them.

Randy Byrd,
Broker at eXp Realty in Santa Rosa, California,

I believe that a willingness to step outside of one's comfort zone is paramount because growth occurs when we embrace the unfamiliar.It involves embarking on a personal journey of growth, which resonates with me as well.

Personally, I embody coachability to the extreme. In the realm of real estate agents, being coachable is essential. In fact, if someone is not coachable or lacks the desire to expand beyond their existing boundaries, we may not be a suitable match. There are other teams that may be a better fit. The key question is whether someone is willing to embrace discomfort, embrace growth, and embark on this journey together.

Bic DeCaro,
eXp Realty, Ashburn, Virginia

A coachable individual possesses self-awareness, recognizes its importance, and willingly embraces feedback as constructive criticism for personal growth. They are accountable for their actions and decisions. This willingness to learn and absorb without constantly trying to modify everything is a key aspect of coachability.

They approach the coaching relationship with the mindset of acknowledging that they have tried things their way and now seek a better way. Their focus is on learning from their coach, rather than constantly tweaking and questioning. As I progressed, I transitioned to different coaches who provided clear guidance and assignments. This structure greatly contributed to my success.

I had a mindset of following instructions and executing the prescribed process without challenging it. Some may call it blind faith, but it was not blind because the coaches I trusted had a proven track record. I placed my trust in individuals who had already achieved success, and by adhering to their guidance, I achieved positive outcomes.

Lindsay Stevens,
eXp Reality, Hudson Valley, New York

To embody coachability, one must embrace accountability. It entails being open to stepping outside of your comfort zone and undertaking tasks that may not always align with your preferences. Taking personal responsibility for the commitments you make and the goals you set is crucial. When interviewing agents, I inquire about their coachability. Are they willing to be challenged? Are they prepared to be held accountable? These aspects hold significant importance.

Self-reflection and self-discovery are closely intertwined with coachability. Coaching involves delving into these areas and being motivated to fulfill necessary actions. It's easy to let tasks linger without taking action, but when I make a commitment, I recognize the need for a high level of accountability. I understand that I must take ownership of my actions and fulfill my obligations, whether it's through personal reflection or reporting my progress to others.

Larry White,
eXp Reality, Houston, Texas

When I help an agent, I put together a business plan for what they want to do. When I think of people who are coachable, I ask for acceptance. Will they allow me to hold them accountable for the things they said they needed to do?

If you're never going to cold call somebody, I don't need to teach you the best script because you're not going to use it. So I build a business plan for what they want to do.

When I think of somebody who is coachable, I ask for acceptance. Will you allow me to hold you accountable for the things that you said you need to do on a daily basis? So a big part of being coachable to me is the willingness to be held accountable and to make minor adjustments. That's because the plan that you put together the first time isn't always going to work because the market changes so fast.

You might have the best mailing campaign that you've ever put together, and if the market shifts, it could be thrown out the window. So we have to be able to adjust and pivot really quickly all by analyzing the numbers. So that's where we have to track and measure.

We have to be held accountable and we have to be willing to adjust. So, in my eyes, being coachable means that you're willing to do these three things: discipline, maintaining a schedule, planning your work, and working on your plan.

CHAPTER 4:

HOW TO ACHIEVE AND EMBRACE SELF-DISCIPLINE?

Self-discipline is a paramount achievement that propels both professional and personal growth. It serves as a pathway to success in your career and brings happiness to your life. The rewards are abundant, but they hinge on your commitment to cultivate or enhance self-discipline and practice your newfound or refined skills daily.

Self-discipline entails the ability to persevere despite distractions or tempting opportunities and to maintain self-motivation even in the face of adversity. It is fueled by determination and yields self-control, ultimately leading to success in various aspects of life, including family and career.

Several barriers may obstruct the path to self-discipline, such as a lack of motivation, procrastination, and everyday distractions. However, with dedication, effort, and training, you can overcome these behavioral hurdles. The key is to prioritize the most challenging tasks and tackle them first.

Contrary to popular belief, discipline is not an innate quality. It is a learned skill that develops through exposure and personal experiences. Often, it emerges from one's environment, whether it be family, education, sports, or other domains where the importance of this skill becomes evident.

There are three avenues to foster self-discipline: positive reinforcement (acknowledging and praising your efforts), negative reinforcement (setting consequences for undesirable behaviors), and restorative reinforcement (correcting and rectifying flawed behaviors).

By embracing self-discipline, you can unlock your full potential, achieve remarkable growth, and lead a fulfilling and accomplished life.

"Discipline is the bridge between goals and accomplishment." —Jim Rohn

---

The Discipline of Time Blocking

Time blocking is a time management technique that involves allocating specific blocks of time for different tasks, activities, or priorities throughout your day or week. It helps you structure and organize your time more effectively, ensuring that you dedicate focused periods to important tasks and avoid distractions. Here's an explanation of how time blocking works:

1. Identify Your Priorities: Start by determining your key priorities and goals for the day or week. Consider both work-related tasks and personal activities that require your attention.

2. Break Your Time into Blocks: Divide your available time into distinct blocks or chunks, typically ranging from fifteen minutes to several hours, depending on the nature of your tasks and preferences. Consider your energy levels, concentration span, and the estimated duration of each task when determining the block lengths.

3. Assign Tasks to Specific Blocks: Assign specific tasks, activities, or categories of work to each time block based on their priority and the level of focus they require. For example, you may allocate a block for email management, another for creative work, one for meetings, and so on.

4. Set Clear Start and End Times: Assign precise start and end times to each time block. This creates a sense of structure and helps you stay disciplined and accountable to the allocated time frame. Avoid extending a block beyond its designated time unless necessary.

5. Minimize Distractions: During each time block, minimize distractions and interruptions as much as possible. Turn off notifications, close unnecessary tabs or apps on your computer, and communicate your availability to others if needed. Create a conducive environment for focused work during these dedicated blocks.

6. Maintain Flexibility: While time blocking provides structure, it's important to remain flexible. Unexpected events or urgent tasks may arise, requiring adjustments to your schedule. Allow for buffer time between blocks to handle unforeseen circumstances or provide yourself with short breaks.

7. Review and Reflect: Regularly review and reflect on your time-blocking approach to assess its effectiveness. Identify areas for improvement, such as tasks that consistently take longer than expected or blocks that need to be adjusted. Adapt your schedule as needed to optimize productivity and efficiency.

"Discipline is choosing between what you want now and what you want most."—Abraham Lincoln

---

Time Block

Step up your productivity game with time blocking!

Here's why time-blocking rocks.

- Improved Focus and Productivity: Say goodbye to multitasking! By dedicating specific blocks to important tasks, you can sky-rocket your progress and accomplish more efficiently.

- Enhanced Time Management: Allocate your time like a pro! Prevent time wastage and give your important tasks the attention they deserve.

- Bye-bye Procrastination: Break tasks into manageable blocks, commit to specific time frames, and become accountable for your progress. Procrastination, who?

- Work-Life Balance, Achieved: Make time for what matters! Dedicate blocks to personal activities and self-care to balance work and life seamlessly.

- Better Workflow and Planning: Visualize your time like a pro! Spot gaps, avoid conflicts, and optimize your schedule for maximum efficiency.

Ready to rock time blocking? Try digital calendars, planners, or productivity apps. Discover your perfect system and make every minute count!

First in your Discipline Is Sticking to your Schedule

1. Boosted Productivity: When you follow a personal schedule, magic happens! It keeps you laser-focused and shields you from pesky distractions. By having a clear plan for the day and sticking to it, you effortlessly dodge interruptions and time-wasters. It's your secret weapon to unleash your full potential and skyrocket your productivity.

2. Crushing Deadlines: In the business arena, meeting deadlines isn't just important—it's a deal-maker. Your personal schedule acts as your trusty roadmap for achieving tasks and projects within those time frames. By sticking to your schedule, you'll wow clients, customers, and colleagues with your unwavering commitment to professionalism.

3. Masterful Planning: Your personal schedule serves as a mighty tool to take charge of your work life. It lets you strategically allocate time for each task, predict how long activities will take, and set realistic timelines for project completion. By honoring your schedule, you become the embodiment of organized brilliance, effortlessly transforming goals into achievements.

4. Stress-Busting and Overwhelm-Smashing: Say goodbye to stress and overwhelm! With a personal schedule in hand, you'll face the day with unrivaled poise and control. By mapping out your tasks and responsibilities, chaos won't stand a chance! Prepare to sail through your workday with a sense of calm and confidence.

5. Pro-level Professionalism: Being a schedule champion is a surefire way to showcase your professionalism and reliability. It communicates that you not only respect your own time but also value the precious time of others. By honoring commitments, you'll build a reputation of trust and credibility, opening doors to endless opportunities and prosperous relationships.

6. Thriving Work-Life Harmony: With a personal schedule, the sweet symphony of work-life balance becomes your reality. It empowers you to manage your time like a maestro, dedicating precious moments to both work and personal pursuits. By honoring your schedule, you'll savor the joys of family, hobbies, self-care, and all that makes life truly fulfilling.

Embracing your personal schedule is the secret formula to conquering time management, unlocking untapped productivity, obliterating deadlines, unleashing planning prowess, annihilating stress, radiating professionalism, and mastering a harmonious work-life balance. So, let your schedule be your guiding light, leading you to triumph, fulfillment, and success in your professional journey.

"We must all suffer from one of two pains: the pain of discipline or the pain of regret. The difference is discipline weighs ounces while regret weighs tons." —Jim Rohn

---

Maybe you Need More Motivation!

The lack of motivation can stem from various causes. Fear of the unknown often leads us to retreat rather than move forward. Uncertainty and lack of clarity regarding goals can also drain motivation, whether due to setting inappropriate objectives or facing challenges that feel overwhelming or trivial. Additionally, adopting a victim mindset and blaming circumstances can significantly impact motivation.

To ignite motivation, break tasks down into manageable parts and acknowledge your progress, giving yourself credit for each achievement. Celebrate even the small victories, recognizing that monumental accomplishments are not built overnight. Often, we tend to overestimate what we can achieve in the short term, but looking back, we realize the multitude of small steps that have brought us to where we are today.

Remember to be kind to yourself as well. Share your progress with a trusted individual who can provide support and accountability, further fueling your motivation.

Sustaining motivation requires pushing beyond your comfort zone and bolstering your confidence. Surround yourself with people who uplift your mindset and envision the great outcome of your goals. The circle of friends or colleagues you surround yourself with plays a crucial role in determining your potential in life.

As the saying goes, "OQP"— Only Quality People. Let go of those who don't elevate you, even though it may be challenging. Over time, you will witness improvements in your thought processes and overall life.

The phrase "only quality people" generally refers to a desire or preference for associating with individuals who possess certain positive qualities or characteristics. It suggests a preference for surrounding oneself with individuals who are considered to be of high caliber, integrity, competence, or moral character.

The term "quality" in this context can vary depending on the specific context or individual using the phrase. It could encompass traits such as intelligence, professionalism, reliability, honesty, expertise, or a strong work ethic. Essentially, it implies a preference for individuals who demonstrate positive attributes and contribute positively to a particular environment, whether it be personal relationships, professional settings, or social circles.

The concept of seeking out "only quality people" is often associated with the belief that the people you surround yourself with can influence your success, growth, and overall well-being. By associating with individuals who possess desirable qualities, one may hope to enhance their qualities and experiences through positive interactions and influences.

In addition, it is highly beneficial to actively seek out and immerse yourself in environments where you find yourself surrounded by individuals who possess a higher level of knowledge and expertise. This deliberate choice fosters an environment of continuous personal growth, igniting the desire to achieve greater success through inspiration and learning from others.

Procrastination

Raise your hand if you can relate to being a procrastinator! I know I certainly can. Procrastination often arises when we are fully aware that there is a task that needs to be accomplished but choose to delay it. It can stem from not knowing what to do or feeling overwhelmed by a new issue or problem. Sometimes, the negative emotions associated with a particular task can also contribute to procrastination.

Distractions play a significant role in fueling procrastination. Our attention is easily diverted by unrelated or distant matters that draw us away from the work that requires our focus. It could be something as simple as a noise, wandering thoughts, the constant buzz of our cell phones, or anything that steals our attention from the task at hand.

Practicing self-discipline is crucial in combating procrastination and achieving success. However, it's important to be aware of the pitfalls that can hinder our progress. As humans, we naturally gravitate towards the path of least resistance, seeking the "easy button." We prefer to avoid difficult tasks, even though deep down we know that taking on those challenges will make our lives easier in the long run. We often find ourselves engaging in small, unrelated activities to avoid tackling the more demanding tasks, requiring a strong dose of self-discipline to refocus our attention where it's needed.

Another factor that contributes to procrastination is the fear of unfamiliar or complex tasks. This uncertainty about where to start or what to do leads us to seek distractions, hoping that inspiration will strike magically. We may spend time rearranging our workspace or engaging in other activities related to our business while avoiding the inevitable task.

Here's a better approach: Set manageable deadlines and create a schedule. Determine specific start times and allocate a set amount of time to work on each task. Increase your focus by setting smaller goals within the larger project. Promise yourself a reward once the task is completed. When reviewing your schedule, make sure to allocate dedicated time blocks for recurring daily tasks throughout the week as a reminder of the work that needs to be done. This technique is known as time blocking.

Identify potential obstacles that may hinder your progress and develop strategies to overcome them. Self-discipline plays a vital role in preventing last-minute issues. As the deadline for a challenging task approaches, anxiety may mount, making it even more difficult to complete the task effectively. By practicing self-discipline, you can maintain a sense of control and produce high-quality results.

Remember, deadlines serve as valuable tools to keep you focused and propel your self-discipline. They create a sense of urgency and provide the necessary energy to pursue your goals. Embrace deadlines as an essential component of setting small, achievable goals. After all, goals without deadlines are mere dreams.

**"The difference between a successful person and others is not lack of strength, not a lack of knowledge, but rather a lack in will."
—Vince Lombardi**

This May Not Be Discipline, However, it May Help: Divide and Conquer

Establish clear boundaries and prioritize tackling the difficult task first. Once you complete the challenging task, you'll experience a significant sense of relief, making the remaining tasks feel easier to handle.

It can be beneficial to experience some level of pressure to dispel the misconception that the task is an insurmountable monster. With time, you can adapt to and handle any situation. Think about how diamonds are formed under extreme temperatures and pressure in the Earth's mantle.

To make a difficult task less overwhelming, break it down into smaller sections that can be tackled one at a time. Set specific time limits, such as working for twenty or thirty minutes before taking a break. This approach allows your subconscious mind to process the situation, and you may gain fresh insights when you return to the task.

Utilize a spreadsheet or planner to hold yourself accountable and keep track of your progress. Checking off completed sections of the project helps maintain focus. Find a planner that suits your needs and preferences, as it can prove beneficial and lead to positive life changes. Additionally, share your project's progress with trusted friends who can help hold you accountable for maintaining self-discipline.

Developing self-discipline requires making it a habit through consistent practice and consciously breaking free from habits that hinder your progress.

Take a moment to dive deep within yourself, exploring your areas of struggle and strengths. You hold the power to turn self-discipline into a reality in your life. It all starts with developing heightened awareness—the pivotal first step toward driving meaningful change. By recognizing and acknowledging the problem at hand, you build the solid foundation necessary to kickstart and sustain transformative actions. Without a profound awareness of the issue, the path toward fostering positive transformation becomes an exhilarating challenge. So, let's cultivate a keen understanding and consciousness of the obstacles that await our attention. Together, we can bring about impactful change.

"We don't have to be smarter than the rest. We have to be more disciplined than the rest." —Warren Buffet

---

Do Not Be Afraid of Failing

As you set sail on the voyage of self-discipline, it's important to acknowledge that failure may be on the horizon. Embrace these failures as valuable lessons. Similar to when a teacher in high school returned your test, highlighting the incorrect answers and guiding you toward the right ones, these mistakes serve as teachers that leave a lasting imprint in your memory.

When you encounter failure, take the time to analyze the reasons behind it and make the necessary corrections. This process not only enhances your motivation for success but also builds resilience and growth.

Remember here's the thing: you don't have to strive for perfection. Let's embrace that because the truth is, nobody's perfect. In fact, chasing perfection might actually stall your productivity. Instead, let's shift our focus to taking that first step, no matter how tiny, and just start on your journey. It's through your consistent effort, unwavering perseverance, and genuine dedication that you'll witness that mind-blowing improvement over time. Trust the process and always remember that progress is a direct result of nonstop practice and learning from the epic adventures that life hands us. Keep challenging yourself, my friend, because, with each step forward, you'll unlock incredible new glimpses of personal growth and achievements you never thought possible.

Seek support from others to make self-discipline an integral part of your being. Having the guidance of an experienced coach can make navigating new territories much easier, as they can show you the way to the future you envision.

Applying Discipline in Business Situations

To steer clear of organizational freefall and pave the way to a thriving real estate business, aspiring owners must prioritize discipline. Unlocking the secret to effective discipline practices in the workplace is the key, and this can be achieved through a myriad of strategies. Think: encouraging positive behaviors, fostering two-way communication, promoting collaboration, providing on-the-job training, and arming employees with knowledge about the ever-evolving real estate market.

Developing a comprehensive plan serves as the roadmap for your team to follow. This plan should outline the rules and expectations, while also cultivating a culture of respect. Clearly communicate the disciplinary plan in writing to ensure everyone is aware of the company's policies. It should be fair and consistent, including behavioral standards and guidelines on how violations of company policy will be addressed.

The disciplinary plan can also incorporate performance improvement strategies, helping manage the performance of team members by setting clear objectives and goals. It's essential to provide avenues for feedback to foster continuous improvement.

Motivate your team members by using the plan to recognize and celebrate achievements. Consider implementing incentives and prizes for hitting goals and demonstrating exceptional performance. Recognizing and reinforcing desired behaviors goes a long way in boosting morale and productivity.

It is advisable to have an attorney review your disciplinary plan to prevent future issues and safeguard your business and its reputation.

Regularly evaluate the effectiveness of the plan and identify areas for improvement. Learning from experience is invaluable, and having a real estate coach who has already navigated similar challenges can provide valuable guidance and support throughout your real estate journey.

"Success isn't measured by money or power or social rank. Success is measured by your discipline and inner peace." —Mike Ditka

---

AROUND THE BLOCK . . .
INTERVIEWS WITH TOP ECHELON REAL ESTATE
PROFESSIONALS ABOUT DISCIPLINE.

Carin Nguyen,

The Carin Nguyen Real Estate Network, Phoenix, Arizona

I have cultivated a strong sense of discipline, which stemmed from my desire for freedom after leaving corporate America. Initially, I viewed freedom as the ability to do whatever I wanted, but I soon realized that this perspective also brought its own limitations and constraints. True freedom, I discovered, lies in being disciplined with my schedule and ensuring that my time is dedicated to the right tasks. It all begins with establishing a time block and committing to it.

However, I recognized that simply having a time block wasn't enough. I had to be honest with myself and evaluate where I was deviating from the schedule, exceeding the allocated time, or neglecting certain tasks. I questioned the importance of the tasks I was ignoring and made a commitment to prioritize them within the designated time block. This ongoing evaluation and adjustment became a continuous process of refinement.

Working with coaches has been instrumental in navigating through these challenges. Coaches help uncover blind spots that may hinder progress. As the visionary of our company, I focus on activities that build key relationships, work on the business through reporting and addressing agents' and clients' concerns, and engage in coaching, training, attraction, and vital conversations with leadership. For tasks that fall outside my area of expertise, I have learned to delegate them to others who are better suited for those responsibilities.

Discipline is a constant journey of self-improvement, and I am continuously refining my approach. By staying focused on high-priority tasks aligned with my vision, I am able to maximize my time and experience true freedom in both my personal and professional life.

Daniel Beer,

Daniel Beer Home Team CEO & Owner, San Diego, California

Every day, I adhere to a consistent waking time and follow a well-structured morning routine. These are the hallmarks of discipline. However, the most significant aspect is integrating discipline into my very identity.

In those challenging moments that we all encounter, when the temptation arises to deviate from our commitments, I have trained myself to respond differently. It is at these junctures where most people stumble and retreat. But I have come to recognize that these moments are actually doorways that we must pass through.

For instance, let's say that I have committed to writing a post on Facebook every day. Initially, I diligently write one post after the other. Yet, at some point, I may encounter a day where I feel a reluctance to engage in this task. It is at that moment that I might start bargaining with myself, concocting excuses and promising to make up for it tomorrow. It is precisely during this critical moment that I must pause and reflect.

Rather than succumbing to the allure of procrastination, I have learned to embrace this moment with anticipation. I recognize it as the defining moment I have been waiting for—an opportunity to rise above and showcase my discipline. It is in these moments that true growth and transformation occur, separating those who persist from those who falter.

By internalizing discipline as part of my identity, I am able to face these pivotal moments with excitement, knowing that they present a chance for me to demonstrate my unwavering commitment. These are the moments that distinguish men from boys, unveiling the strength and resilience that lie within.

Katharine Loucaidou,
Real Estate Group, Bolton, Ontario, Canada

I possess a high level of discipline and self-motivation, which fuels my drive to succeed. I don't rely on external sources to motivate me because I apply enough pressure on myself to propel me forward. I have cultivated this mindset out of necessity, particularly during a period when I had multiple jobs, and two young children, and was pursuing a master's degree in the evenings while living in Europe.

To navigate through my demanding schedule, I implemented a time-blocking system that encompassed every aspect of my life. Although the tasks may not always be completed in a specific order, the practice of time blocking has become deeply ingrained in me. It has become a powerful tool that enables me to effectively manage each day and accomplish what needs to be done.

Time blocking has been a constant companion throughout my journey, serving as a reliable structure that helps me stay on track and maximize my productivity. Its influence has extended beyond that challenging period and continues to be a guiding principle in how I approach each day. By adhering to this practice, I am able to maintain a sense of organization and tackle tasks efficiently, even in the face of a demanding schedule.

Randy Byrd,
Broker, eXp Reality, Santa Rosa, California

I come from a military background, and that has deeply influenced my approach to coaching and teaching. I run a real estate agent boot camp where I prioritize discipline and instill it in every aspect of my work. I constantly evaluate my level of discipline, and currently, I would rate myself at 9.1 out of 10. To me, a perfect ten means having no excuses and allowing nothing to hinder progress. However, achieving this level of discipline involves finding a balance and making necessary adjustments along the way.

Discipline is not just a concept I talk about; it is something I embody. It is a non-negotiable value for my team members, coaching clients, and the entire organization of 900 individuals. They didn't join to have someone dictate their actions; instead, they expected me to lead by example.

I firmly believe in living by the principles I preach. When I hold coaching calls and emphasize accountability and discipline, I must demonstrate these qualities myself. I set high standards for myself to ensure I can uphold the disciplines I expect from others.

By setting clear boundaries and establishing specific guidelines, we create a framework that enables us to achieve the best possible results. These boundaries serve as a roadmap to success, allowing us to stay focused, motivated, and disciplined throughout our journey.

Bic DeCaro,
eXp Realty, Ashburn Virginia

My family instilled a strong sense of discipline and maintained strict standards. I observed my parents' unwavering dedication to their work and business, which served as a powerful example for me. Their approach to discipline was clear—when they set expectations, we followed them without question, and it proved to be effective.

In addition to my parents, I also learned from my siblings, who played a significant role in my upbringing. As part of a large family, my older siblings took on the role of secondary parents. Respecting their authority was ingrained in me, and I learned the importance of not challenging them. My brother, in particular, became a father figure to me, and I valued his guidance and teachings.

The combination of observing my parents' discipline and respecting and learning from my siblings contributed to my understanding and appreciation of discipline. These experiences shaped my character and influenced the way I approach life and work. Discipline became a fundamental aspect of who I am, guiding my actions and decisions.

Lindsay Stevens,
eXp Reality, Hudson Valley, New York

Discipline runs deep within me. It is an integral part of my DNA, ingrained through my upbringing and personal experiences.

Growing up, I was surrounded by two entrepreneurial parents who owned an insurance brokerage. Witnessing their hard work and dedication, I learned the value of discipline firsthand. Despite their busy schedules, they always made time for our family, demonstrating the importance of balance and presence.

From a young age, I embraced athletics and became involved in running. Starting at the age of twelve, I pursued running as a passion, which continued throughout high school and even during my sophomore year at UMass Amherst. Being an athlete further honed my discipline, teaching me the significance of commitment, perseverance, and pushing beyond my limits.

In addition to my athletic pursuits, I had a unique upbringing around boxing due to my father's involvement. Though not a competitive boxer himself, my father was deeply immersed in the sport. I spent much of my childhood in and around the boxing ring, witnessing the dedication and mental toughness required in this demanding discipline. My father's words, "Shake it off," became a mantra for resilience and taught me the importance of bouncing back from setbacks.

These diverse influences have shaped my character and fostered a steadfast discipline within me. The lessons learned from my parents' work ethic, my athletic endeavors, and the boxing world have contributed to my unwavering determination and ability to rise after falling. Discipline is not just a trait I possess; it is an integral part of who I am and how I approach life's challenges.

Larry White,
eXp Realty, Houston, Texas

I'm probably now, an eight and a half. I used to be a twelve. I don't have as much leverage anymore. I know I could make more money every single day. There are more important things than money to me.

So, I wake up every morning at 5:00 or 5:30 at the latest. It's breath work, it's meditation, it's gratitude all before my kids wake up. Because once other people start waking up, they start pulling for your time. So it's so important to me because I see how much I get out of it. I have to do that before the business starts.

And then I cook breakfast for my kids every morning. I take my dog for a walk. I walk my kids to the bus stop. And then I take an hour of planning to see what the three to four most important things in my day need to be. What are the most dollar-productive behaviors? And then, every day, three o'clock, maybe sometimes four o'clock, I'm done.

And because I'm picking up my kids from school; I'm taking them to football or dance because those are the things that are important to me.

So again, I've made the income, I've done this, I've made the right investments by budgeting and by doing this and that. So the goal has changed, the target has changed where I'm not worried if I will make this much or that much.

It's not financially motivating to me anymore. Time is more important than money.

CHAPTER 5:

YOU WON'T SUCCEED WITHOUT IMPLEMENTATION!

Now that you've equipped yourself with valuable tools for real estate success and personal happiness, it's crucial to weave them into a well-defined plan and incorporate them into your daily routine. This is the moment of implementation where you take effective action on your ideas and plans to conquer your tasks!

Once upon a time, in the realm of basketball, there existed a legendary team known as the Millers. Fueled by raw talent and a fiery love for the game, these individuals possessed an unbreakable bond. And leading this brotherhood was none other than Coach Pete, a master strategist with a knack for turning weaknesses into opportunities.

One fateful day, while dissecting their upcoming opponents, the Millers unraveled a hidden pattern within their foes' defensive armor. Coach Pete's eyes gleamed with insight, and a mischievous grin painted his face. He concocted a game-changing play, a concoction of intricate movements, impeccable timing, and split-second decisions.

In the sacred halls of the practice gym, the Millers gathered, eager to bring their coach's vision to life. Hours bled into one another as they fine-tuned their positions, honed their moves, and etched each step into their muscle memory. With relentless determination, they drilled until perfection became their second nature.

And so, the day of reckoning arrived. The Millers took the court, their hearts pounding with anticipation. Patiently they awaited the opportune moment, like lions in the tall grass, ready to pounce. The ball flew through the air, landing in the hands of the point guard, who triggered the sequence like a maestro commanding an orchestra. In a symphony of athleticism and precision, the Millers moved as one, flawlessly executing their meticulously choreographed dance.

The opponents stood frozen, jaws agape, as the Millers weaved their magic. Desperation and disarray swept through their ranks, like a tempest raging in the night. The weakness discovered and exploited had become their nemesis, and the Millers reveled in their newfound advantage. The arena shook with the euphoria of the crowd, witnessing the culmination of vision, preparation, and unadulterated brilliance.

And so, the Millers etched their names into the annals of basketball lore. Forever it shall be known that on that magical night, they transcended the boundaries of the ordinary and became legends woven into the fabric of the game.

In the upcoming chapter, we will delve into the crucial aspect of execution. This topic holds great importance as the mere act of implementation, without the necessary follow-through, can often be a recipe for failure. By exploring the intricacies and nuances of effective execution, we can uncover the key ingredients required for success.

Implementing your newfound knowledge can feel overwhelming, but there's no need to despair. This challenge applies not just to the aforementioned example but to many complex concepts we encounter. Often, it is easier to acquire knowledge than to put it into practice. To navigate this process effectively, consider writing down the steps and procedures involved. Many experts recommend online note-taking or journaling as methods to keep your thoughts organized and externalize them from your mind. Think of it as creating an external brain. By documenting your ideas and delving into unfamiliar territory, writing can bring clarity while reinforcing what you have learned, why it is relevant, and how it can be applied to your business and daily life.

To take it a step further, let your ambitions seamlessly blend into your daily hustle. These aspirations should revolve around small, attainable wins that, when consistently conquered, pave the path to extraordinary outcomes. Craft your goals with the SMART framework: specific, measurable, achievable, results-focused, and time-bound. As for your calendar or schedule, employ the power of time blocking. Allot dedicated blocks of time for activities that bring the utmost value to your journey. Remember, time is your most prized possession. By skillfully managing and protecting it, you unlock your ultimate productivity and conquer your wildest dreams.

"A strategy, even a great one, doesn't implement itself."
—Jeroen De Flander

Develop a Comprehensive Business Plan

As a licensed real estate agent, you hold the keys to your own small business empire. But here's the deal, my friend: a mere checklist won't cut it. You need a comprehensive business plan that sets the stage for your success. So, let's start by dreaming big. What are your wildest aspirations? While financial goals are important, let's get specific: How much moolah do you want to rake in and take home? Armed with these numbers, we can reverse engineer your path to victory by calculating closings and volume needed to hit those targets.

Your well-crafted business plan is like a magical bridge, connecting your grand vision with your short and long-term goals. Within its realms, you'll find a realistic budget and an assertive marketing strategy, all enclosed within a defined timeframe. But wait, there's more! We're talking SWOT analysis, my friend. It's time to assess your strengths, weaknesses, opportunities, and threats, injecting a shot of reality into your plan. Buckle up and get ready to conquer the real estate landscape, considering all the internal and external factors that may impact your business.

Embarking on the real estate journey? Set yourself up for success by crafting a comprehensive business plan that encompasses your financial goals, marketing strategy, and SWOT analysis.

To navigate the ever-changing landscape, dive into the multiple listing services (MLS) and uncover thriving areas, cool markets, and promising opportunities.

Stay up-to-date by immersing yourself in market research, studying the MLS regularly, and exploring multiple communities and neighborhoods.

When diving into the real estate market, keep a close eye on the average number of days a property stays on the market and the corresponding price trends. Don't forget to watch for new listings in your target area and compare them with previous years, months, or weeks. This will give you a crystal-clear view of market conditions and help you make smarter decisions.

But that's not all! Delve deeper and research your rivals, gaining valuable insights into their performance and the number of agents in your chosen real estate sector and location. Social media platforms can be your secret weapon, giving you a window into your competitors and uncovering untapped market opportunities.

"There's a difference between interest and commitment. When you're interested in doing something, you do it only when it's convenient. When you're committed to something, you accept no excuses; only results."
—Kenneth H. Blanchard

And don't forget the most important element: passion. Align your passion with the countless opportunities in real estate, using your strengths to shine in your chosen field. With determination and expertise, you'll carve your path to success. So get ready to make your mark in the world of real estate!

To effectively reach your potential clients in desired markets, it's crucial to understand their unique needs and preferences. Dive deep into their world and pinpoint the specific segment they belong to—whether they're eager first-time homebuyers, individuals longing for more space, or any other defined category.

But don't stop there! Uncover valuable insights about where people are moving from and heading to within these markets. Consider life-changing events that shape their housing decisions—from divorce, job changes, and family formation to expanding their households.

Yet, remember: your business plan is never set in stone; it's a living, breathing document. Continuously review and update it, ideally every ninety days or on a quarterly basis, seeking necessary tweaks and improvements. By diligently honing and refining your plan, you'll adapt to the ever-evolving market landscape and pave the way for your business to triumphantly achieve its goals. Let the journey begin!

> ### "A strategy, even a great one, doesn't implement itself." —Jeroen De Flander

---

Prioritize your Business Plan

In the world of business planning, trying to tackle everything at once is a recipe for overwhelm and disappointment. Instead, let's focus on this game-changing strategy: prioritize the most critical aspect and pour your energy into it, while ensuring you follow up effectively. Once you have conquered that goal, smoothly transition to the next priority on your list. Break it down into short-term goals, swiftly activate them, and watch your business dreams come to life. Remember, the key is to resist the urge to juggle everything simultaneously. Dedicate your time and attention to each goal individually, and conquer them one by one like a boss!

Crafting a business plan can feel like an intimidating mountain to climb. But fear not! It's the cornerstone of success for any entrepreneur worth their salt. By refining your ideas, mapping out strategies, and carefully weighing the pros and cons of each aspect, you'll unlock the true potential of your venture. With clear goals lighting your path, you'll confidently embark on your entrepreneurial journey, knowing that greatness awaits.

Now, let's talk about that sense of accomplishment! Start small by knocking out those quick tasks and triumphantly crossing them off your to-do list. Or, inject some joy by tackling tasks you genuinely enjoy. Trust me, it'll help quell that looming anxiety of an endless list of responsibilities.

Personally, I love conquering the toughest tasks early in the day. It's like a badge of honor that propels me forward, radiating confidence throughout the day.

"Change is easy to propose, hard to implement, and especially hard to sustain." —Andy Hargreaves

---

Attention all real estate aficionados! To thrive in this digital era, you must establish a visible online presence. Embrace the power of the Internet and social media, as more and more people rely on them for their real estate needs. Embrace the limelight and wave goodbye to being the "secret agent." Instead, take the reins and actively seek out potential clients, rather than waiting and hoping they stumble upon you.

Ready to stand head and shoulders above the competition? Here's the secret sauce: Create an exceptional experience for your customers. Show them you genuinely value their business. Tune in to their needs, go the extra mile, and leave them with that warm fuzzy feeling of utmost satisfaction. In a fast-paced world, prioritizing customer care and putting their needs first will give you an undeniable edge that'll leave a lasting impression.

Now, let's dive into the world of first-time homebuyers. These newcomers need your guidance like never before. Give them a comprehensive understanding of the real estate process and current market conditions. By discussing important market trends, you'll establish yourself as the ultimate expert, equipping them with accurate information for their crucial purchase. Paint a vivid picture of each home's key features, such as location, size, amenities, and other relevant details. This level of detail instills confidence and helps them make informed decisions. And hey, don't forget to share your insights on local areas, schools, and community dynamics. It'll make a world of difference and ensure they feel right at home. Lastly, don't underestimate the power of educating them about financing options.

Empower them to make savvy, well-informed investment choices. By holding their hand through every step of the process, you'll become their trusted guide and leave them feeling confident and supported.

"Implementation is a discipline, and good companies make it a core part of their competencies." —Louis Gerstner.

Conduct a Reality Check

Embark on your journey toward your goals with a strong connection to yourself. Stay centered and focused on your internal compass as you confidently navigate toward your desired destination.

Take a moment to reflect on your life's purpose, your "why." Does it still resonate with the same clarity and meaning as when you first discovered it? Have you gained fresh insights along the way? Let your "why" be the unwavering force that ignites your motivation every single day. Cultivate self-discipline and hone your time management skills to optimize your productivity.

Should you find yourself being overly critical, it's time for a change of gears. Remember, perfection isn't always necessary for success. In fact, pursuing perfection can hinder progress and breed negativity. Shift your focus to progress, taking one step at a time. Embrace self-compassion and maintain a positive attitude as you work toward your goals.

Stay connected, nurture self-compassion, and foster a positive mindset. These will empower you to make significant strides toward your desired outcomes. Approach your journey with enthusiasm and determination as you strive for greatness, always wearing a smile.

When starting a business, consider the value of hiring a coach. A coach can provide valuable guidance and support, helping you save time and avoid common mistakes. With their assistance, you'll embark on a streamlined and successful entrepreneurial journey.

Let the fire within you light the way to your dreams. Embrace the challenges, cherish the victories, and savor every step of your remarkable adventure.

"The world needs dreamers and the world needs doers. But above all, the world needs dreamers who do."
—Sarah Ban Breathnach

Building an Implementation Plan

As Winston Churchill once wisely stated, "Planning is everything, plans are nothing." These words resonate with undeniable truth, for without a well-constructed map, we are destined to lose our way. Ignoring the importance of thoughtful planning is akin to paving a path toward failure. So, let us pause and chart our course, readying ourselves for the thrilling journey ahead, knowing that the rewards for our efforts will be grand.

However, amidst our meticulous preparations, let us not forget the unpredictable twists and turns that life often brings. These paradoxes of existence remind us that even the most carefully crafted plans can be disrupted by unforeseen detours. Picture yourself excitedly packing for a year-long-awaited trip to the Bahamas, only to have your dreams crushed by a sudden hurricane decimating your reserved hotel. Or imagine the thriving housing market tempting homeowners to sell, only to see their hopes dashed by an unforeseen economic downturn. At once, the solidity of our plans crumbles, revealing the capricious nature of life.

In the face of such unpredictability, it is the awareness of the unexpected that ignites our spirits and propels us forward. It is in adapting, in embracing the challenges that life throws our way, that we truly come alive, for it is from the ruins of shattered plans that new and exciting opportunities often arise, leading us on unimagined paths of growth and fulfillment.

So, let us plan meticulously, but let us also embrace the twists and turns that come our way, knowing that within their unpredictability lies the richness and vibrancy of life.

While meticulous planning is undoubtedly crucial, it's equally vital to embrace adaptability and resilience when unexpected challenges arise. Accept that adjustments may be needed along the way, and be prepared to recalibrate your course when necessary. By cultivating a flexible mindset, you'll gracefully navigate detours, propelling yourself closer to achieving your goals.

"Genius is 1% inspiration and 99% perspiration." — Thomas Edison

---

Embracing change, despite its inherent challenges, can unlock hidden advantages and pave the path to soaring success amidst the ever-evolving business landscape.

As you construct the roadmap for your real estate business, remember that it's no ordinary static document. Rather, it's a vibrant and dynamic entity, subject to constant evolution. In reconciling the paradox of a living plan, prioritize maintaining crystal-clear vision in both your thoughts and actions. Let your unwavering clarity guide you toward triumph and triumph propel you forward.

Embrace the vast array of available technologies as your allies in shaping and executing your plan. Tap into the power of tools like Word, Excel, Evernote, Monday, Grow, and PowerPoint to breathe life into your strategic vision.

"Ideas are a dime a dozen. People who implement them are priceless." —Mary Kay Ash

---

Your implementation plan should be a well-crafted masterpiece. It should be packed with vital details like comprehensive task descriptions, defined start and completion dates, clear deadlines, estimated durations, assigned individuals, and a carefully planned schedule for project meetings. And let's not forget the preliminary budgets for each task; every penny counts!

Remember, flexibility is the key to success. As your project unfolds, be prepared to adapt and navigate uncharted territories. Build flexibility right into your plan, allowing adjustments to smoothly integrate into the mix.

Now, let's talk about the secret sauce—organizational order and agility. They are your superpowers! By maintaining a pristine order and gracefully adapting to unforeseen circumstances, you'll ensure your plan's success. Also, don't forget to constantly analyze feedback and proactively make necessary adjustments. This will pave the way for the smooth execution of your project within the designated timeline and budget.

A few keys to implementation . . .

- **Analyze:** Embark on your journey by delving deep into thorough research. Dive into the currents of your market area, exploring its past and present conditions. Uncover hidden gems by surveying the dynamic business landscape, conversing with key players, and anticipating potential risks. Stay in tune with the economic climate, be proactive and well-informed. But don't stop there, keep your gaze fixated on the horizon, as the future unfolds, ensuring a smooth navigation for your business.

- **Adapt:** Embrace the power of delegation! Tap into your resources—staff, spouse, friends—and assign tasks that align with your strategic plan. If delegation isn't possible, fine-tune and prioritize the vital tasks that truly demand your personal attention. Don't forget to identify potential risks to your business and devise strategies to overcome them. And always, always consider the second-order consequences and evaluate your risk tolerance. If the risks are manageable, forge ahead confidently!

- **Overcome:** Take the time to carefully fine-tune your plans, making necessary adjustments and refinements along the way. Assess the resources at your disposal and anticipate what lies ahead. Then, strategically allocate your resources to tackle the most pressing aspects of your business head-on. Craft a comprehensive roadmap that encompasses your research, planning, and implementation efforts. For seamless execution, leverage tools and templates offered by specialized companies to bring your strategic plans to life!

Embrace these transformative concepts to unlock a whole new level of change implementation. Delve into the intricate process of turning ideas into reality and gain a profound understanding. Navigate the complexities of change with confidence and finesse, achieving impactful outcomes in your endeavors.

"Vision without action is a dream. Action without vision is simply passing the time. Action with Vision is making a positive difference."—Joel Barker

---

AROUND THE BLOCK...
INTERVIEWS WITH TOP ECHELON REAL ESTATE
PROFESSIONALS ABOUT IMPLEMENTATION.

Carin Nguyen,
The Carin Nguyen Real Estate Network, Phoenix Arizona

I excel at creative and innovative ideas, but admittedly, I struggle with taking them from A to Z. To solve this, I start with the simple act of taking notes. With my trusty notepad, I jot down all my thoughts and review them to identify action items. I'm not the type to go back through my notes and highlight them, so I transfer those action items to a to-do list. And to ensure I don't neglect this important step, I include a time block in my schedule dedicated to note-taking. I use a Trello board to sort and organize the action items, and when it's time to execute, I have a built-in process that makes it all happen.

Daniel Beer,
Daniel Beer Home Team CEO & Owner, San Diego, California

After attending events, the abundance of great ideas can be overwhelming. Deciding what to prioritize from the list of ideas and putting them in the right order can be the biggest challenge. To avoid getting caught up in confusion, it's important to figure out which ideas to implement and which to keep aside for later.

One way to ensure you don't miss out on good ideas is to make a file of them, revisiting it periodically to check if it's the right time to execute them. But focusing on just one or two ideas at a time can eliminate the inertia caused by overwhelming to-do lists.

Take the time to differentiate between the fabulous ideas and the ones that are vital to meeting your goals. Only then will you avoid being caught in priority confusion. It's essential to hold ourselves accountable to ensure we make progress on our goals.

Katharine Loucaidou,
Real Estate Group, Bolton, Ontario

I am incredibly disciplined and self-motivated; it's always been a necessity in my journey. I discovered my passion and began attending seminars and mastermind groups, carefully choosing which would accelerate my progress.

One thing I learned is that every time you attend a seminar or hire a coach, you're in a different place on your journey. So, while the information may not seem immediately applicable, it can be implemented down the road when you're ready.

Being a member of Masterminds for seven years has enabled me to be in a room filled with high-level people and learn so much. However, during the first two years of attending, there was such an information overflow that I would leave feeling more depressed than when I arrived. But by the third year, I realized that everyone was at a different level.

It was then that Jon suggested that I do Facebook Live every morning for three years when I had my brokerage. Asking why no one was doing video, I delved deeper to succeed in real estate. And being that type of person—where if I'm doing something, I'll do it thoroughly—I went in all in. Not once, but several times to gauge the result. Remember, results do not come overnight; it takes a while to build up an audience.

Randy Byrd,
Broker, eXp Reality, Santa Rosa, California

I recently attended a two-day intensive session, spending ten hours each day with Michael Reese and Woods Davis. We delved into funnel hacking and building follow-up systems, exploring how to capitalize on Facebook ads. Being an avid note-taker, I transitioned to using the remarkable Notepad for the first time and ended up with a whopping ninety-six pages of notes from the event.

After returning home, I went through the notes and selected no more than ten percent of them to focus on initially. From there, I narrowed down to about ten pages of valuable information and actionable items, which I documented in a new set of written notes. I continued filtering until I had identified three or four key actions to implement, out of the ninety-six pages.

This process is like a funnel, where I take a large amount of notes (ninety-six pages in this case) and gradually filter out valuable information, prioritizing it until I am left with a few actionable items. Each action item is further broken down into steps, with consideration for which task has the greatest impact or is the easiest to complete.

Given the varying timelines of the action items, some may take longer than others to implement, but I am all about momentum. So, this is my method of making progress even when presented with a vast amount of information.

Bic DeCaro,
eXp Realty, Ashburn, Virginia

Attending conferences is an invigorating experience—like stepping into a candy store as a child eager to be showered with treats. However, before attending, I often have a list of objectives that I aim to tackle—issues that may have been hindering my progress or growth. My aim is to acquire the solutions that I seek, a technique I learned is the "do doing done" method. Driven as I am, I obsess over these objectives, enforcing a strict to-do list approach. Over the years, the objectives have multiplied, and I steadfastly integrate them into my workflow, often leaning on my trusted production partner and executive assistant.

While affirmations are critical, I found that leveraging my business required stepping back from buying and selling so that my production partner could expand and improve the results of my referrals. Thanks to this setup, I am free to lend my attention to problem-solving only when necessary. Picture us as doctors; if there's an issue, I'm the specialist who tackles that specific problem, and then I step aside to let my team do what they do best. While I no longer attend all inspections or walkthroughs, I facilitate negotiations and implement marketing strategies for our clients.

Lindsay Stevens,
eXp Reality, Hudson Valley, New York

I'm not the one for implementation. That's where our sales manager and my husband, Bruce, who oversees operations, come in. At present, my focus is entirely on sourcing and recruiting talent. I dedicate at least an hour every day to expanding our team, as managing this sizeable group is my top priority.

Over time, we've implemented various initiatives that we've either quickly realized won't work or haven't had the chance to follow through on executing. Nevertheless, framing and executing these initiatives has been valuable in identifying where we need to focus our energies, be it through pushing ahead with an initiative, altering it, or moving toward a completely different direction.

Larry White,
eXp Realty, Houston, Texas

Anytime you go to a sales conference or a coaching call, it can be overwhelming. My coach taught me this way back in the day. You eat an elephant one bite at a time because you can't implement everything. This is where you create that business plan in actionable steps to accomplish it.

So generally when I bite off something two to three steps at a time. What are the first two or three things I need to do to accomplish this goal? If I can't do that maybe it's the wrong goal. Then I have to re-evaluate why am I not doing this. I deem this as important. I set up these steps. Why am I not following through with this?

It's really breaking it down to actionable items and once you've developed that then creating the next ones and the once ones and he next ones. I view it as if we're in Los Angeles and our flight takes off, three degrees of separation takes us to Miami or New York. It's not this huge jerk of the wheel. It's these small little pivots. And that's what you have to do with our business plan. So small actionable items every single week, taking steps forward over and over and over again.

Now look back in six months and look at how much I've accomplished.

CHAPTER 6:
EXECUTION IS CRUCIAL!

The success story of Walt Disney exemplifies the significance of not only ideation but also resolute execution. Disney showcased an incredible talent for creating iconic and beloved characters, such as Mickey Mouse, Donald Duck, and Goofy, which deeply resonated with audiences and laid the groundwork for the enduring Disney brand.

Aside from his creative genius, Disney was also a technological innovator. He always pushed the boundaries of animation and introduced groundbreaking advancements in the industry. This innovative spirit took Disney's creations to new heights and set the stage for future developments in animation.

Walt Disney didn't just create cartoons; he went a step further and brought us Disneyland in 1955, the world's very first modern theme park. Talk about setting the stage for a major milestone in entertainment and tourism! And that's not all—this success led to the birth of Walt Disney World in Florida, followed by expansion to international locations. Disney truly became a trailblazer in the theme park industry, making magic happen worldwide.

Throughout his career, Walt Disney always stressed the significance of quality, innovation, implementation, and execution. He was all about paying close attention to every little detail, making sure the storytelling was top-notch, and creating immersive experiences that truly captured the hearts of the audience. This commitment to excellence became the foundation of Disney's success and set the bar for the entire entertainment industry.

Walt Disney's success can be attributed to a few key factors. First, his ability to create enduring characters that resonate with generations. Second, his innovative use of technology pushed the boundaries of storytelling. And let's not forget about the establishment of those theme parks that brought the magic to life. He didn't stop there, though. Disney expanded into various entertainment sectors, leaving an enduring legacy. But what really sets Disney apart is his unwavering commitment to quality and his determination to execute his vision. That's what turned Disney into the entertainment empire we know and love today.

"Vision without execution is hallucination." —Thomas Edison.

As you may glean from the remarkable life of Walt Disney, it is imperative to acknowledge that mere implementation alone is insufficient. True progress and achievement stem from the deliberate and skillful execution of ideas, strategies, and plans. By dedicating oneself to the meticulous process of translating vision into reality, one can unlock boundless opportunities for success and leave an indelible mark on the world.

Failing to execute our strategies puts us at risk of falling short of our desired outcomes, goals, and potential. It's like a football player diligently following a play, but unable to convert it into desired results. They drop the pass, miss the block, or fumble, ultimately failing both themselves and the team.

Let's remember: Execution is the vital link between intention and accomplishment. It's the key to achieving success!

Similarly, imagine having a delicious recipe at hand and meticulously gathering all the fresh ingredients. However, in the rush to create a masterpiece, you neglect to execute the directions accurately. As a consequence, what was meant to be a delectable dish turns into a messy, unsatisfying creation, ultimately resulting in a wasteful outcome. This setback not only squanders your valuable time but also incurs unnecessary expenses and consumes precious resources that could have been put to better use.

In the realm of real estate, many agents may implement pay-for-leads campaigns, but without proper execution, such as calling the leads and using effective sales scripts, the desired sales won't materialize. If an agent advertises an open house but fails to adequately prepare, build rapport, and follow up with interested parties, the intended results will not be achieved. Implementation alone cannot guarantee success; it is the execution that truly matters.

According to Harvard Business School, without proper execution, around ninety percent of businesses fail to achieve their strategic goals. And, when you are a real estate agent, you are running a small business. So, this applies to you. While executing what we have implemented can be challenging, it is not impossible. It requires consistent effort and a steadfast commitment to taking action. Execution is not meant for the lazy or those seeking shortcuts.

When we understand the importance of execution and truly commit to following through with our plans, amazing things can happen! It sets us up for greater success, growth, and fulfillment. By embracing the discipline and effort needed for effective execution, we pave the way to achieving our strategic goals and unlocking our true potential.

> "Ideas are easy. It's the execution of ideas that really separates the sheep from the goats." —Sue Grafton

Empower your Team Members . . . if you have them

According to my father's wise advice, repeating the same actions in the same manner will yield the same outcomes. To achieve the desired results, the execution of implemented ideas must be driven by the overarching goal, rather than merely following a daily to-do list. If we continue doing what we've always done, we will always get what we always got. We will not grow to reach our desired destination. We must implement and execute new ideas and explore uncharted territories.

To ensure all team members are on board with the strategic goals of the business and understand how their contributions fit into the big picture, as a leader, it's crucial to create a clear and inspiring vision. Instead of overwhelming them with a laundry list of tasks, you need to determine the necessary steps and execute them effectively. Your vision is the compass guiding your business and employees toward a brighter future. While the vision can change in as little as ninety days, it's important to strike a balance and avoid constant flux. After all, people crave some sense of stability and direction on their journey.

Unlock the true potential of your staff by guiding them to focus on essential tasks that drive their assigned goals. Empower each team member with specific objectives, minimizing bureaucratic hurdles and mundane busywork. Answering the fundamental question of who is responsible for what and by when sets clear expectations. But remember, it's not about building a rigid bureaucracy; it's about unleashing your team's hidden talents. Embrace delegation to elevate your growth.

"The key is the clarity on the obstacle and consistency of disciplined execution on the critical drivers."
—Kieth Cunningham

When individuals are empowered, they develop a sense of ownership over their roles and responsibilities. This ignites a drive to achieve the intended outcomes, fostering a workforce that performs with the dedication and accountability of business owners. By aligning their efforts with the strategic goals of the organization, you'll witness magnificent growth unfold before your eyes.

"Execution is the chariot of genius."
—William Blake

Measure and Monitor Performance

To gauge your success and progress toward your performance goals, you need to rely on real data from key performance indicators (KPIs). These indicators validate your advancement with objective evidence.

When considering KPIs, don't forget to look at both leading and lagging indicators. Leading indicators predict outcomes while lagging indicators track past performance. And don't forget about milestones! They offer insights for better decision-making and help measure progress.

To choose effective KPIs, follow the SMART formula. Make sure they are specific, measurable, attainable, realistic, and time-bound. And remember to regularly review and update your KPIs to stay current with the growth and changes in your business, market, and customer base.

Dashboards have become essential tools in our industry. They visually represent whether you're on track or off track.

In the real estate industry, KPIs cover a wide range of aspects like real estate and commercial sales, management, leasing, and property development. For real estate agents, specific KPIs might involve keeping track of their calls, conversations, texts, emails, appointments, and the number of signed and pending contracts. The KPIs that are of utmost importance primarily make use of lagging indicators. In the realm of real estate, these indicators are more evident and straightforward. They include the number of contracts signed and completed closings, measured in units, as well as the volume and gross commission income, gross revenue and net profit.

"Without execution, 'vision' is just another word for hallucination." —Mark V. Hurd

---

Execute your Marketing Strategy

The Internet is a vast realm of marketing opportunities, and your business website serves as the gateway to make an indelible first impression. But rather than attempting a DIY approach, why not entrust your vision to a professional web designer who can breathe life into your ideas? Take the time to interview multiple designers, exploring their skills, creativity, and working style to find that perfect match.

Remember, communication is the key! Clearly articulate your objectives and expectations for your web presence. Once you've chosen a designer, request them to wow you with three captivating concepts. This way, you can easily narrow down your preferences and ensure your website is an embodiment of your vision.

But it doesn't stop there! To truly create a website that stands out, you need the support of a marketing company proficient in developing print, photographic, and video materials aligned with your goals. Seek expertise in crafting engaging blog posts and other collateral for your website. And don't forget to review and approve the content they provide before moving forward.

And the journey doesn't end once your website is up and running. It's vital to keep your content fresh and updated regularly. Showcase your successes and achievements with monthly updates that captivate and inspire!

Alternatively, you may explore the option of engaging real estate-specific companies who possess the expertise to meticulously plan and execute an outstanding website that aligns perfectly with your vision and objectives. This way, you can ensure that every aspect of your online presence exudes professionalism and leaves a lasting impression on your target audience.

"Execution is a specific set of behaviors and techniques that companies need to master in order to have competitive advantage." —Ram Charan

---

Here are some additional strategies to amplify your real estate marketing efforts:

1. Leverage social media platforms such as Facebook, Instagram, and LinkedIn to showcase your property listings and engage with potential buyers. Use visually compelling images and videos to capture their attention.

2. Collaborate with local influencers or bloggers who have a strong following in your target market. Partnering with them can help increase your brand exposure and attract a wider audience.

3. Offer virtual tours or 3D walkthroughs of your properties to give potential buyers a realistic and immersive experience. This can save time for both you and the buyers, as they can narrow down their choices before scheduling in-person visits.

4. Host informative webinars or virtual workshops to share your expertise in the real estate industry. This can position you as a trusted authority and help build credibility with your audience.

5. Implement email marketing campaigns to stay in touch with potential buyers and nurture your leads. Send out regular newsletters, market updates, and exclusive property listings to keep them engaged and informed.

By incorporating these strategies into your real estate marketing plan, you can enhance your visibility, engage with your target audience, and ultimately drive more leads and sales.

**"Plans are only good intentions unless they immediately degenerate into hard work."
—Peter Drucker**

Accountability Is Crucial

Accountability is an indispensable element for successfully executing what you have implemented. While discipline plays a crucial role, seeking assistance from others to hold you accountable is perfectly acceptable.

As the leader of your real estate business, it is your responsibility to establish goals and outcomes, both for yourself and your organization. If you have a team or brokerage, ensuring that individuals are accountable for their contributions to the bottom line is essential.

In order to maintain a high-performing team or brokerage, effective leadership entails regular discussions about purpose, goals, culture, values, and results. These conversations provide a clear sense of direction and foster a collective mission among your staff.

> **"Success doesn't necessarily come from break-through innovation but from flawless execution."**
> **—Naveen Jain**

Successful real estate leaders and teams engage in ongoing communication, sharing information and insights as the business evolves over time. They actively offer and receive feedback, allowing for adjustments based on changing insights and external influences. Without such open communication, teamwork diminishes and the execution of implemented strategies suffers. Ultimately, your organization's culture plays a significant role in shaping how you handle these circumstances.

Adaptability is crucial, and troubleshooting is necessary to identify and rectify any issues that may arise within the business. Just like an aircraft encountering thunderstorms during a flight from Los Angeles to New York City, adjustments need to be made to the flight plan to navigate around disruptions.

Changing conditions in the business environment, such as the recent and impactful Covid-19 pandemic, often necessitate a re-evaluation of procedures and potentially even goals. We all vividly remember the disruptions caused by widespread shutdowns. Many businesses were forced to close their doors for months, and some are still grappling with the aftermath.

Executing what you have implemented can be demanding, so seeking assistance and support will make the process more manageable.

> **"Strategy is a commodity, execution is an art."**
> **—Peter Drucker**

AROUND THE BLOCK...
INTERVIEWS WITH TOP ECHELON REAL ESTATE PROFESSIONALS ON WHAT THEY MAY NOT HAVE EXECUTED ON...

Carin Nguyen,
The Carin Nguyen Real Estate Network, Phoenix, Arizona

I may not be the person responsible for executing ninety-nine percent of the tasks within our organization. Recognizing this allows me to relinquish control and understand that taking responsibility means having the power to effect change, rather than blaming others for not fulfilling their duties. Ultimately, it comes back to me as the one who hired or allowed them to continue without progress.

To gain clarity on the execution aspect, I have found the Entrepreneurial Operating System (EOS) to be tremendously helpful.

While there is currently a lot of industry chatter about execution, we managed to achieve significant success last year without putting in a great deal of effort. However, there is one aspect that weighs heavily on my mind at the moment: our plans to become home wealth advisors or consultants.

In my opinion, our greatest strength lies in providing clients with a wide range of options and being knowledgeable about those options, even if we don't present every single one. It's important to let clients decide what is best for them without imposing our own beliefs.

Unfortunately, our big launch for home wealth advisors or consultants last year did not materialize as planned. Looking back, I realize it faltered because I was attempting to handle everything on my own, which was an unrealistic expectation. I lacked clarity on who would handle content creation, how the rollout would happen, and the associated deadlines.

The project was not fully developed, and this lack of a proper process caused it to fall through. It is essential to have a well-defined process in place to ensure its success. Currently, we utilize Trello as our project management tool, which allows us to create boards and manage projects effectively.

Daniel Beer,
Daniel Beer Home Team CEO & Owner, San Diego, California

Every day, my routine involves three core activities: recruiting, content creation, and meetings with my team leaders.

In terms of our business operations, we successfully implemented a system called Raven for managing all our off-market listings. We dedicated considerable time and effort to developing this system, ensuring its effectiveness, and training our agents on its usage. Once the system was created, rolled out, and taught to our team, we unfortunately neglected to provide ongoing communication and support for it. However, I want to emphasize that the system itself is fully functional and complete.

Katharine Loucaidou,
Real Estate Group, Bolton, Ontario

I successfully implemented various initiatives, but I struggled with the execution aspect, mainly because it drained my energy and wore me down.

Being an independent brokerage in an industry dominated by branded competitors posed significant challenges for me, especially as a woman. I was surrounded by brands within a fifty to hundred-kilometer radius, with no other women managing real estate or owning brokerages. Opening my independent brokerage as a woman was like swimming against the current.

For five years, I faced constant resistance and pushback. Not only did I have to recruit based on my unique value proposition, but I also had to counter the appeal of joining established brands. The lack of visible results combined with the ongoing pushback gradually took a toll on my motivation and resilience.

To streamline my activities and manage my time effectively, I have designated specific days for different responsibilities. Mondays and Tuesdays are dedicated to coaching, while Wednesdays are focused on my team. On Wednesdays, I prioritize content creation for all my platforms related to my real estate business.

Despite juggling multiple roles, including running a real estate team, coaching, hosting a podcast, and creating content, I recognize the need to find a better balance and avoid spreading myself too thin.

Randy Byrd,
Broker, eXp Reality, Santa Rosa, California

When we implement a new strategy and begin executing it, there may come a point where we realize it isn't working or it no longer aligns with our objectives. This realization has shifted my perspective on prospecting. While I used to rely heavily on forward-based prospecting for agents, clients, buyers, and sellers, I now believe that attraction-based approaches are more effective in today's world. As a result, I am fully embracing webinar funnels for both attraction and social media awareness.

Recently, we implemented a five-day-a-week calling structure, but upon reflection, I recognized the need to pivot rather than completely abandon it. I have devised a new plan that conflicts with the existing schedule, so the pivot allows us to adapt and make the necessary adjustments. It's not like starting to paint a house and then giving up halfway because of laziness. It's more like painting half the house in gray and realizing that we actually wanted it in brown, so we go back and make the necessary changes.

My execution plans are relatively straightforward. I utilize an app, which we developed specifically for real estate. It follows a thirty-day cycle, similar to the concept of 75 HARD. Completing these thirty-day cycles is currently a primary focus for us. Additionally, I find inspiration from books like "*The 12-Week Year*," which provide valuable insights on effective implementation and execution.

During a recent podcast by Ed Mylett, he shared a powerful concept: "I'm going to crush you because I have three days in every one day. You have one eight-hour day, and I have three eight-hour days." This concept highlights the importance of maximizing productivity and efficiency in our execution efforts, allowing us to achieve more in less time.

Bic DeCaro,
eXp Realty, Ashburn, Virginia

Well, I've implemented certain strategies, but I admit that the execution hasn't been as strong as I would have liked, particularly when it comes to my email campaigns. I've found myself trying to achieve perfection in the messaging, which has hindered the effectiveness of my email campaigns.

As a team leader, visionary, and rainmaker, I have two primary responsibilities. First, I am actively involved in production myself. Second, I lead a team of salespeople who ensure that our business is consistently taken care of and our agents are effectively serving our clients. The frontline members of our team are always my top priority.

While the operations team is vital and plays a crucial role in supporting our operations, it's important to recognize that it's the frontline sales efforts that generate the revenue to sustain our operations. Therefore, we must ensure that our agents have a strong support system in place, including virtual assistants who play a significant role in assisting them.

My main focus is on frontline lead generation, ensuring that our team receives a consistent flow of leads. Additionally, I take on the responsibilities of a sales manager and handle marketing initiatives. I work alongside a production partner and a business development manager, making a total of seven of us who are dedicated to supporting our agents in various roles.

Lindsay Stevens,
eXp Reality, Hudson Valley, New York

When it comes to the growth of our business, we've implemented numerous strategies, but we've also realized that not all of them can be effectively executed. Through this process, we learn and discover which initiatives are worth pursuing further and which ones may require adjustments or a different direction altogether. It's important to evaluate and determine the best path forward before committing to full execution.

Delegating tasks used to be a challenge for me, as I believed that only I could complete them successfully, which is a common mindset for many people. However, I quickly learned that this was not true. In fact, those who took on the tasks often executed them even better than I would have. This realization allowed me to tap into the superpowers and expertise of others, leading to improved experiences and better outcomes. Now, I have become much better at delegating and executing tasks, understanding the importance of scaling and enhancing the overall effectiveness of our operations.

Larry White,
eXp Realty, Houston, Texas

I can say the common theme for me when I don't implement or execute is that it didn't align with my goals. But I wasn't passionate about it. So if I'm not passionate, similarly, again, if you are never going to make a cold call, I don't need to teach you the script that allowed me to set seventeen listing appointments in three weeks. It's irrelevant. Because you're never going to use it.

You go to these motivational seminars, conferences, or conventions, and learn about weight loss as you think life would be so easy if I did that. But if you don't want to workout, if you don't want to change your eating habits, are you interested, committed or obsessed? If you are committed, then one step forward. If you are obsessed, you will find a way to get it done.

CHAPTER 7:

THE MAGIC HAPPENS WHEN YOU TRACK AND MEASURE!

Congratulations on successfully implementing and executing your real estate business! Now, let's take a step back and reflect on your achievements. What goals have you reached, and what remains to be accomplished? This introspection is crucial as it lays the foundation for monitoring your efforts and measuring your outcomes—key ingredients for real estate success.

By adopting a systematic approach to track and measure your progress, your business transforms into a mathematical model. This clarity empowers you to make informed decisions on which actions to pursue and which ones to abandon, propelling your business growth.

Remember, it's important to keep your data quantifiable, using numerical values whenever possible. This allows you to observe trends over time. For example, by tracking the number of leads generated from a specific marketing drive, you can evaluate its effectiveness and decide on its future applicability. Tracking and measurement not only optimize your financial resources, but they are also integral to thriving in the competitive real estate industry.

"If you can't measure it, you can't improve it."
—Peter Drucker

Establishing a robust tracking and measuring system helps you identify potential hurdles and take preemptive action to mitigate any irreversible damage. It optimizes the allocation of your time and resources, ensuring standardization, consistency, and ongoing enhancements. Following Pareto's Law, focus on the top twenty percent that generates eight percent of your bottom-line results. This systematic approach allows you to stay updated on your real estate business's progress and make necessary modifications along the way.

A well-designed tracking and measuring blueprint provides the insights needed to make informed decisions that can significantly amplify your profits. It reveals patterns and trends, shedding light on the effectiveness of your business strategies. This knowledge is vital as your business landscape evolves, allowing you to make calculated decisions and refine your approach based on experience and historical lessons.

Prompt assessment of your tracking and measuring system at the end of each quarter is crucial. Many businesses find quarterly reviews beneficial as they offer incremental monitoring of progress. Additionally, this approach aids in strategic resource allocation and goal setting for the upcoming quarter. To ensure accurate tracking, define specific goals and expected results for each assessment period. Once the goals are set, scrutinize the collected data and compare it against benchmarks or previous quarters. This comparison will help you evaluate the effectiveness of your strategies and make necessary adjustments.

Now, let's delve into the key parameters needed for your tracking and measurement tasks. Here are some essential metrics prevalent in the real estate industry. Let's elevate your real estate business to new heights!

Key Real Estate Metrics to Track

Key performance indicators (KPIs) are super important metrics that help you evaluate how your business is performing. To collect the right data, you have to have a well-thought-out plan. This plan should cover five to seven KPIs that you think are crucial for success.

When selecting your KPIs, it's a good idea to have a mix of leading and lagging indicators. Leading indicators are like fortune tellers, giving you a heads-up on trends or shifts in the market or your business. They help you look ahead. Meanwhile, lagging indicators show outcomes that happened too late to influence your actions.

The cool thing about leading indicators is that they predict future success and give you a chance to adjust your action plan. But, they can be a bit tricky to interpret. On the other hand, lagging indicators are easier to measure and are less likely to cause disagreements.

Some leading indicators to start with are:

- Number of leads generated per month
- Calls
- Contacts
- Appts
- Contracts written
- Pending marketing effectiveness

Lagging indicators:

- Closed units

- Closed volume

- Closed commission

- Gross revenue

- Net profit

"What gets measured gets managed."
—Peter Drucker

More specifics on some business KPIs are below:

Sales KPIs are crucial metrics that help assess how well your sales team is performing. They include things like the number of new contracts secured and their monetary value. You can also track the number of qualified leads in your sales funnel, the time and resources dedicated to sales follow-ups, the average time it takes to convert leads, and the net sales percentage or dollar value.

Financial KPIs give insights into the financial health and growth of your business. They cover areas like revenue growth rate, net profit and gross profit margins, operational cash flow, current accounts receivable, and inventory turnover rate. Monitoring these KPIs helps you understand the financial performance and profitability of your company.

Customer KPIs focus on measuring customer satisfaction and loyalty. These metrics involve tracking the number of retained customers over a specific period and the percentage of market share they represent. Customer KPIs help you evaluate the effectiveness of your customer retention strategies and assess your market position.

Operational KPIs assess the efficiency and productivity of your business operations. These indicators may include measuring the time it takes to fulfill an order, the time invested in marketing activities, employee satisfaction scores, and the employee turnover rate. By monitoring operational KPIs, you can identify areas for improvement, streamline processes, and enhance overall operational effectiveness.

"Data beats emotions." —Sean Rad

Marketing KPIs evaluate the success of your marketing efforts in driving brand awareness and generating leads. They might involve tracking monthly website traffic, the number of keywords ranking in the top ten search engine results, the frequency of blog posts published each month, and the number of qualified leads generated. Analyzing marketing KPIs helps you assess the effectiveness of your marketing strategies and optimize your campaigns for better results.

Tracking and analyzing these different types of KPIs provide valuable insights into various aspects of your business's performance. With this data, you can make informed decisions, identify areas for improvement, and drive overall business growth and success.

Maintaining Data Security

When it comes to data security, it is crucial to avoid repeating the same actions to prevent the loss or inadvertent compromise of valuable information, or falling prey to malicious actors. To strengthen your tracking and measuring plan, it is important to incorporate best practices for data security. These practices can include using two-factor authentication whenever possible, ensuring strong password security with a combination of letters, numbers, and characters, regularly backing up data and storing copies in separate locations or cloud storage services, implementing measures to protect against malware and cyber threats, keeping an eye on user access logs and watching out for suspicious activities, establishing a system for quick data restoration in case of attacks or system failures, using encryption protocols for sensitive information, regularly reviewing and updating security policies, having cyber insurance to mitigate potential losses, and educating your team about the importance of cybersecurity and best practices.

By implementing these measures, you can significantly enhance the security of your data, reduce the risk of unauthorized access or data loss, and protect your business from potential cyber threats. Taking proactive steps to safeguard your information and educating your team on security practices will help strengthen your data security framework.

"In God we trust, all others must bring data."
——W. Edwards Deming

Technology for Agent Motivation

Maintaining the enthusiasm and drive of real estate agents within your firm is a crucial determinant of your business's prosperity. A shared metrics dashboard can effectively stimulate agents, offering a quick overview of their pivotal metrics and performance data. This dashboard also enables agents to gauge their accomplishments in comparison to their peers, thereby fostering a competitive spirit.

Offering incentives for reaching specific objectives or milestones can further enhance motivation among agents. Incorporating the latest technology into your company can also bolster agent enthusiasm. Tools like virtual tours, mobile applications, and other interactive platforms simplify real estate dealings more than ever, allowing agents more time to concentrate on their clients, which in turn boosts their motivation.

Establishing an open-door communication policy aids in maintaining agent motivation by offering a platform where agents can express their viewpoints, raise issues, and receive constructive feedback from management. This cultivates trust between the agent and the company, resulting in elevated motivation levels. Simultaneously, it contributes to shaping the unique culture within your company.

Real estate agents actively seek companies that not only foster a great culture, but also provide opportunities for production, recognition, and comprehensive training. These factors play a vital role in attracting and retaining top talent in the industry.

When it comes to tracking and measuring progress, incorporating gamification can be a game-changer. By turning tasks into challenges, such as increasing closings through appointment competitions, you can motivate agents and create a competitive environment. Tracking agent appointments with clients allows you to correlate the percentage of appointments to property listings and sales.

By leveraging gamification and performance reports, you can not only motivate agents but also objectively evaluate their performance. This combination helps drive productivity and creates a dynamic and thriving work environment in the real estate industry.

"Having a specific measurable plan enables you to have the optics required to see the deviations in real-time and course-correct accordingly".
—Kieth Cunningham

Gamification is a powerful tool for keeping your team motivated. By setting goals and offering rewards for achieving them, such as bonuses or prizes based on levels of success, you foster friendly competition among employees and incentivize them to work harder. This not only boosts individual performance but also cultivates team spirit and camaraderie among coworkers. Furthermore, gamification streamlines your organizational efforts by allowing you to track performance over time and determine the most effective strategies for your team.

In addition, the online dashboard revolutionizes your business operations and sales strategy in real-time, eliminating the need for IT consultants. It also generates comprehensive performance reports that enable you to accurately gauge the productivity of your agents. This invaluable data empowers you to identify areas in need of improvement and design better strategies for success. While gamification motivates agents and fosters a competitive environment, the performance reports provide an objective evaluation of staff performance.

"If you torture data long enough, it will confess to anything." —Ronald Coase

---

Generating Client Leads

The generation of leads is a key component in attaining success. After all, businesses need clients to prosper. Effective marketing techniques and invaluable word-of-mouth referrals are the main sources of lead creation. However, it's crucial to remember that generating leads is just the beginning of the journey to success, and there's no such thing as an excess of leads.

Transforming leads into prospective buyers or sellers involves arranging an appointment at a time and location that suits the potential client. The meeting serves as a platform for personal interaction, so recommend a meet-up and allow your unique personality to make an impact.

Post-meeting, it's imperative to follow up quickly and express gratitude for their interest. This not only exhibits professionalism but also aids in fostering a positive rapport, which could lead to potential future business engagements.

While having a multitude of leads might seem beneficial, the true picture is somewhat different. It essentially comes down to how these leads are utilized. Many agents invest in leads that, unfortunately, pile up and go unused, thus impeding their potential effectiveness. The key is to focus on the quality execution of the leads you already possess, rather than relentlessly seeking more.

Ensure effective tracking of the leads generated and their respective outcomes by vigilantly overseeing their numbers and resultant transactions.

Understanding how your leads find you and identifying the channels that generate them is essential. Whether these are through your website, social media platforms, advertisements, or referrals, knowing the source will help you allocate your marketing resources more efficiently.

"The most important thing is to be able to see your business in numbers." —Aaron Patzer

---

Overcoming Obstacles

Various obstacles can significantly affect your business, and pricing is no exception when it comes to your listings. Is the property priced appropriately—not too high or too low? Surfacing the right balance is key.

One key metric to track—the number of days on the market—to determine if a property is priced properly. You must also know the overall market average days on the market. For a property that has been too many days on the market, potential prospects might conclude that the property owner is eager to sell, maybe even desperate, and some potential buyers might think there is something very wrong with the property. On the other hand, a property that moves quickly could be seen as highly desirable and might have hidden advantages. Knowing this information can help you plan your marketing strategy accordingly.

When it comes to listings, I like to take a look at the three C's that are crucial for selling a home.

They are:

- Cost

- Condition

- Convenience

- We discussed the cost or list price above.

When it comes to the condition of a home, ensuring it sells for top dollar requires meticulous attention to detail. By meticulously assessing and addressing any maintenance or cosmetic concerns, and by presenting the home in the best possible light, sellers can create a captivating first impression that resonates with potential buyers and motivates them to make competitive offers. Remember, every small improvement contributes to maximizing the overall value of the home and its potential sale price.

"Without data, you're just another person with an opinion." —W. Edwards Deming

---

The convenience of showcasing a home is a crucial factor influencing both the speed and selling price. Easy access to the property not only facilitates potential buyers and their agents in viewing it promptly but also allows for a more in-depth exploration of its unique features, leading to a greater understanding of its value and potential.

The discrepancy between the asking price and the selling price serves as a valuable metric to gauge the percentage difference between the two. It is commonplace in the real estate industry for the sale price to fall below the initial asking price. This KPI plays a vital role in accurately pricing the property, capturing the percentage difference between the asking and selling prices. Typically, this KPI reflects a modest variation, ranging from three to ten percent.

Refinements for Daily

Incorporate these tracking and measuring methods into your daily routine. Assess what you have achieved or failed to achieve, and refine your metrics to allow for improvements in the subsequent quarter. Your personal motivation, or 'why,' will bolster your drive and sharpen your focus. Keep an eye on the changes and outcomes to ensure alignment with your quarterly targets. The consistent accomplishment of these goals is a major marker of success.

"The goal is to turn data into information, and information into insight." —Carly Fiorina

---

While it's crucial to bear in mind that metrics can illuminate patterns, they don't necessarily provide the complete picture. Other elements, such as market dynamics, seasonal changes, customer feedback, competitive scenarios, and industry fluctuations, should also be taken into account.

By tracking your revenue growth on a monthly and quarterly basis, you can glean invaluable insights into the financial efficacy of your actions. This allows you to identify and seize opportunities for enhancing income and broadening your business scope. It empowers you to make informed choices that can positively affect your net earnings. Through detailed observation and analysis of your revenue trends over time, you can fine-tune your strategies and judiciously allocate resources to stimulate sustainable expansion and achievement.

Numerous alternative techniques exist to ascertain if you're applying the most effective targets and measurement metrics for your business in a proactive way, thereby giving you a competitive edge. In such instances, availing the counsel of a person who has previously navigated similar obstacles can be extremely beneficial and of immeasurable worth.

AROUND THE BLOCK...
INTERVIEWS WITH TOP ECHELON REAL ESTATE PROFESSIONALS

Carin Nguyen,
The Carin Nguyen Real Estate Network, Phoenix, Arizona

I'm always this tracking and measuring nerd, you know? I totally geek out over Excel spreadsheets. I mean, I don't necessarily love filling them out, but man, I just love seeing all that juicy data! You won't believe it, but I still remember it being called the number analyzer. From the early days of my business, having that thing filled out for our coaching calls and really having that great understanding and pulse on everything has just been ingrained in me.

So let me tell you what kind of stuff I look at. First off, it's the lead measures, the important ones, you know? Like how many leads are streaming into the business and then how many appointments are set and actually met. Those are key indicators. And, oh boy, past that, I dive into all these awesome multi-year trends. I love seeing how we stack up against our competitors, you know? And don't even get me started on per-person productivity. That's gold!

Now, I'm not all about seasonality, but you better believe I'm all about comparing year over year. I mean, Phoenix doesn't swing too wildly with seasonality. Why? Well, because we have multiple locations! So, yeah, I keep a close eye on our agents' performance. The last quarter? Oh, it's always one of our hot topics!

Daniel Beer,
Daniel Beer Home Team CEO & Owner, San Diego, California

We utilize two tools: Follow Up Boss and Salesforce. Key metrics include vital signs, new leads, and gross margin (also known as company retained dollar). These are the primary indicators. Additionally, we focus on listings signed and appointments booked. When reviewing the scorecard, I prioritize certain elements and disregard the rest of the conversation.

On a weekly basis, I carefully examine the dashboard. Every day, I track pending items. Looking ahead to 2023, our goal is to sell 760 homes, and currently, our gross sales goal is $38 million.

Katharine Loucaidou
Real Estate Group, Bolton, Ontario

My husband introduced me to the importance of tracking and measuring. As someone experienced in management positions, he constantly emphasized the significance of knowing my numbers and understanding where my business was coming from. At first, I was unsure and lacked this knowledge. It was then that he created an Excel spreadsheet and urged me to share the details of my deals. "Tell me where each one came from," he would inquire.

Through this process, I discovered that a remarkable seventy percent of my business in the first and second years was generated from open houses. He emphasized the need for me to be in front of more people, as that was the key to driving my business forward.

But as I began incorporating videos into my strategy, I observed a fascinating shift in my business dynamics. It soon became evident that a significant seventy percent of my business was now originating from Facebook, which was quite astonishing. From that point onwards, I started diligently tracking every aspect of my business, and it truly opened my eyes to new possibilities.

Randy Byrd,
Real Estate Agent and Coach, eXp Realty, Dayton, Ohio

When I started coaching, I quickly grasped the importance of tracking and measuring. In my initial years, I experienced tremendous success in real estate, achieving 338,000 GCI in my first full year. I consistently maintained a high level of production and dealt with units, without truly measuring the value of relationships and referral returns. It wasn't until I received coaching and started tracking and measuring that I realized the true ROI of my efforts. Now, every aspect of my business is quantified.

Let me demonstrate. If you tell me how many deals you want to achieve, we can work backward from there, just like we learned during just like our time coaching together. Let's assume the industry average is forty deals. If your goal is to reach a hundred deals, that's equivalent to having 4,000 conversations per year, mathematically speaking.

This method allows us to extrapolate your targets to a monthly, weekly, and even hourly basis. I find the numbers game fascinating because, by understanding your metrics, we can identify areas for growth. For example, I recently had a client who had been consistently achieving twenty deals per year for the past three years and couldn't seem to break through. Upon further investigation, it became clear that they weren't aware of their numbers. As soon as we pinned down their metrics, we were able to devise a plan to reach new heights.

By tracking and measuring, you gain invaluable insights that can drive your success.

Bic DeCaro

& Associates, eXp Realty, Ashburn, Virginia

Fortunately, I had the opportunity to learn through Enterprise. They trusted me to open up an office in Roanoke when I was just twenty-three years old, which was quite crazy. But it allowed me to gain valuable experience in various aspects, including understanding financials and metrics. While I'll admit I didn't always follow through perfectly, I appreciated being able to gauge my progress and set goals for myself. Those were important to me because I have a competitive nature and wanted to know how I measured up.

Later on, thanks to my coach's guidance, I delved deeper into dissecting metrics. Before that, though, I focused on the basics of tracking and measurement. We have vital indicators in place, and we rely heavily on our Zillow Flex System, which is excellent for tracking. It encompasses various aspects, such as appointments, calls, offer rates, and the number of submitted offers turning into successful closings. If we were generating numerous offers but not closing deals, it indicated that we needed to improve our offer-writing skills. Similarly, if we were going on many appointments but not receiving offers, it meant we needed to enhance our appointment approach.

In the grand scheme of things, I believe all these aspects are essential, especially in the beginning. I used to place excessive focus on conversion, wondering where the breakdowns were occurring. But now, I've come to realize that conversion naturally follows when each preceding step is executed successfully.

Lindsay Stevens,
eXp Reality, Hudson Valley, New York

At the team level, we are actively engaged in tracking our progress. We have implemented contests that promote accountability, resulting in multiple teams participating in contests this month. Our focus is on tracking and measuring are key metrics such as appointments set and tracking offers written Through gamification and incentives, we foster friendly competition among agents to encourage tracking and measurement of these vital activities. We diligently track various actions including dials, text messages, emails, and conversations, recognizing their significance in driving conversions.

Although we have always had teams and a CRM in place, I must admit that I was initially reluctant to fully embrace them. However, I have come to realize the importance of being held accountable myself. This process has given us a valuable opportunity to emphasize the significance of these systems. As I witness the growth of new agents who utilize these systems as intended, I am amazed at the pace at which their businesses thrive compared to the twelve years it took me to build mine.

Larry White,
eXp Realty, Houston, Texas

I can say the common theme between implementing and executing was that it didn't align with my goals. But I wasn't passionate about it. So if I'm not passionate, similarly, again, if you are never going to make a cold call, I don't need to teach you the script that allowed me to set seventeen listing appointments in three weeks. It's irrelevant. Because you're never going to use it.

You go to these sales calls, oh, my gosh, life would be so easy if I did that, if I weighed less. But if you don't want to workout, if you don't want to change your eating habits, are you interested, committed or obsessed?

If you are committed then one step forward. If you are obsessed, you will find a way to get it done.

During my third year in business, the market crash took me by surprise. Feeling like a big shot, closing an impressive 22 to 24 deals annually, I was coached by Mike Ferry, the esteemed father of Tom. Our conversation took an unexpected turn as he casually mentioned having clients who closed more deals in a month than I did all year. It was mind-blowing!

Prompted by Mike, I reevaluated the 40 deals I had worked on over the past three years. To my astonishment, around 80 percent of them (approximately 32 deals) came from past clients and my center of influence, even though I barely interacted with them. It hit me hard. I realized I had been investing all my time and energy into a client group that wasn't generating much business.

In the following year, I decided to abandon calling expired listings and for sale-by-owners (Fizbos). Instead, I dedicated about an hour and a half each day to reconnecting with past clients, my center of influence, and people in my phone contacts. The results were staggering—I went from 22 deals to an impressive 64 in just one year. It was a transformative experience that opened my eyes to a whole new world of possibilities.

CHAPTER 8:

IF YOU DON'T HAVE A PLAN, YOU'LL BE LOST!

When it comes to achieving your financial objectives, it's crucial to effectively reach and educate your target customers about your services and accomplishments. This visibility is key for the growth and success of real estate teams, brokers, and agents. And to maintain this growth, incorporating a few key elements into your annual business plan is essential.

Think of your business plan as your guiding star, providing a vivid vision, ambitious goals, and specific directions for the year ahead. It should include financial goals, strategies for generating leads, initiatives to boost your brand's reputation, tactics for gathering client testimonials, and clear objectives for the next twelve months.

But here's the thing, the financial environment can be unpredictable. That's why flexibility is crucial. Be ready to adapt and make alterations as needed to tackle any emerging challenges. And remember, it's a good practice to review and modify your plan every ninety days to keep it relevant and effective.

While your annual business plan is indispensable, it's also adaptable. It helps you stay focused on your overarching vision, but it's natural that it will evolve throughout the year. However, try to avoid frequent changes to maintain consistency.

Setting goals is a vital part of your plan. Aim for goals that inspire and motivate you, while also being realistic and achievable. Breaking them down into quarterly targets can give you a more manageable structure. Just like the spokes of a bicycle wheel provide stability, these targets keep you on track. Regular reviews will help you identify areas for improvement or adjustment.

If you're feeling unsure about where to start, no worries! We'll dive into the business planning process together and provide you with all the guidance you need.

"Plan for what is difficult while it is easy, do what is great while it is small."
—Sun Tzu, ancient Chinese military strategist

Business Plan Components

Your annual plan revolves around your business plan, which is an important document to have. It all starts with an executive summary, which is like a quick snapshot of your business. You'll talk about who you are, what you do, and what makes you stand out in the real estate market. Think of it as an appetizer to entice potential investors or partners. If you only do this, you will be ahead of ninety percent of all other real estate agents.

In your detailed business plan, you'll describe your company in more depth. This includes your mission, vision, and the strategic objectives you're striving to achieve. Here, you can explain what sets you apart from your competitors and what makes you special in the real estate market. After that, comes the market analysis where you'll dive into the dynamics of the real estate market. You'll identify trends, growth patterns, and potential opportunities. It's important to show that you truly understand the market and have the insight to navigate its challenges.

When developing your business plan, it's also crucial to analyze your competition, however, this is not one hundred percent necessary for a real estate professional. If you are a team or brokerage, study who they are, what they're doing well, and where they fall short. This will help you find ways to differentiate yourself and attract agents.

Describing your real estate services in detail is key. Whether you specialize in residential sales, commercial leasing, or property management, clearly articulate what you do. This will help potential clients understand what you offer and how you can help them.

Your marketing and sales strategies are what fuel your company's growth. Outline how you plan to attract, retain, and expand your customer base. These are mostly leads for the real estate sales professional or potential agents for teams or brokerages that are looking to recruit. Consider using various tactics like digital marketing campaigns, online leads, networking events, your sphere of influence, and referral programs.

"By failing to prepare, you are preparing to fail." —Benjamin Franklin,

---

When you are a team or brokerage, in the operational plan, you'll cover the day-to-day aspects of running your company. Detail your organizational structure, the roles and responsibilities of your team members, and your management processes. This shows stakeholders that your company has a strong and capable team to execute its mission. It is highly recommended to include your leadership team when developing your plan.

Financial projections are also essential to your business plan. They showcase your expected revenue, costs, and profitability for the coming years. It's important to be realistic but also show ambition, demonstrating that your company is financially viable. With real estate business plans, you may be able to find excellent templates to assist.

To make your annual and quarterly plans a reality, it's crucial to clearly assign roles and responsibilities to your team. Regular progress checks and problem-solving sessions help keep everyone on track. Open and clear communication with your team and stakeholders is key to keeping everyone informed and fostering a sense of shared ownership in the future success of your company.

Business Planning Process

Perform a situational analysis using the SMART method, goals, and objectives that are specific, measurable, achievable, relevant, and time-bound. Include a situational analysis and conduct marketing research. Develop a strategic roadmap for implementing your plan and monitor your progress.

As time goes on, you must adjust your plan. But when? The answer is anytime, anything in your market changes, when current economic conditions change, or when change occurs in your business operations or sales staff. These course corrections allow you to effectively allocate your resources, reassign staff responsibilities, enhance accountability, and monitor and evaluate your business progress.

These are what make your business plan a living document and a crucial tool that will serve you well.

> "Plans are only good intentions unless they immediately degenerate into hard work."
> —Peter Drucker

Business Planning Techniques

When it comes to real estate, conducting a Strengths, Weaknesses, Opportunities, and Threats (SWOT) analysis can be a game-changer. This strategic planning tool helps you understand your business's internal and external environments, allowing you to create effective growth strategies and manage risks. Here's a breakdown of how it applies to real estate:

- Strengths: These are the internal aspects that give your real estate business a competitive edge. Think of it as your secret sauce—it could be your stellar reputation, experienced agents, strong client and vendor relationships, or unique marketing strategies that set you apart. Recognizing these strengths will help you leverage them to attract more clients and dominate the market.

- Weaknesses: These are the internal factors that could hold your business back. It could be a lack of brand recognition in a new market, limited resources, a small client base, or struggles to keep up with market trends and technologies. Identifying these weaknesses allows you to come up with strategies to overcome them and improve your overall operations.

- Opportunities: These are the external factors that work in your favor. It could be a booming housing market, shifts in demographics driving demand for specific properties, new legislation benefiting your business, or technological advancements that simplify your operations. Recognizing these opportunities helps you set the right goals and strategies to capitalize on favorable conditions.

- Threats: These are the external factors that pose challenges to your business. It could include a volatile housing market, tough competition, regulatory changes, rising interest rates, or gloomy economic forecasts. By identifying these threats, you can develop contingency plans to lessen their impact and safeguard your business.

Conducting a SWOT analysis allows you to take a comprehensive look at your real estate business. By understanding your strengths and weaknesses, you can fine-tune your operations and stand out from the crowd. Recognizing opportunities and threats helps you navigate market dynamics, empowering you to make informed strategic decisions for long-term growth and sustainability.

"A clear vision, backed by definite plans, gives you a tremendous feeling of confidence and personal power."
—Brian Tracy

Alright, the next crucial step is to set some measurable and achievable objectives for your real estate business. Trust me, this is super important! Why? Well, these goals will help you stay on track and keep a timeline for your business, while also showing you how far you've come. So, aim for realistic targets that match your business capacity and market dynamics.

Now, when you're setting these objectives, make sure they can be measured. I mean, they have to be clear, specific, measurable, have a timeline, and something you can actually track. Imagine you're in an endurance race, like a fifty-mile bicycle race in the autumn. Your long-term goal is to be among the top five, right? Well, to get there, start by setting shorter-term objectives. Like, cycling five miles per day in the first week of summer, and then bumping it up to ten miles per day in the second week. By the week before the race, you'll be hitting fifty miles per day, no problem!

The same thing goes for your real estate business. Set objectives that you can actually measure, like the number of properties listed, properties sold, new leads you have generated, or the total commission generated in a quarter. And hey, as you make progress and the market changes, don't be afraid to raise the bar a bit . . . or maybe you were too ambitious and you need to adjust!

Remember, your real estate business is a mix of your passion, purpose, and the concrete KPIs you've collected. These KPIs give you a clear picture of how your business is doing over time. You know, metrics like leads generated, cost per lead, calls made, appointments set, contracts written, revenue earned, and all that jazz. When your annual review rolls around, these KPIs will show just how well you've been doing.

"A goal without a plan is just a wish."
—Antoine de Saint-Exupéry

Alright, so how do you achieve all of this? It's all about keeping an eye on things, doing regular assessments, and being organized with your records. Use analytics tools to track your KPIs, have team meetings to discuss progress, and be ready to adjust your strategies based on what you learn. Basically, make a cycle of continuous improvement in your business by setting smart goals and using your KPI data to guide your decisions.

Implementing your Business Plan

With all the effort you have dedicated to perfecting your business plan, now is the opportune moment to put it into action. Start by sharing your plan with your coach, mentor, team leader, or other significant stakeholders in your business, both internally and externally. These stakeholders can include individuals, groups, or organizations that may or may not have a personal or economic interest in your business and its performance. You can consider external stakeholders as creditors, customers, business owners, trusted advisors, or mentors, while typical internal stakeholders may include partners, shareholders, and staff.

To ensure effective communication and alignment, schedule a joint meeting with your staff to provide an overview of the plan along with its specific details and goals. Additionally, make time to meet individually with each staff member to gather their input and address their questions regarding their respective duties and goals. By fostering understanding and accountability, you empower your team to contribute to the success of the business.

Another valuable practice is conducting quarterly meetings with your staff to evaluate the achievements and areas needing improvement from the previous quarter. This allows you to make necessary adjustments and modifications to the annual business plan based on the feedback received. By sharing the attained measurements with your staff, you foster transparency and keep everyone informed of the progress.

"Always plan ahead. It wasn't raining when Noah built the ark." —Richard Cushing

---

While implementing your annual business plan, you may encounter challenges that require attention. These challenges can include unclear or vague goals, insufficient market research or analysis, limited involvement of key stakeholders, and underestimation or overestimation of timelines and resources. It's important to address these challenges promptly and adapt to changing circumstances, understanding that people have different inclinations when it comes to adapting to new situations.

By actively making adjustments and course corrections, your annual business plan can truly become a successful and ever-evolving document that guides your business toward success.

Enter the Dashboard

In order to maintain and enhance the speed and performance of your real estate business over time, it is crucial to incorporate the use of technology, specifically a real estate metrics dashboard. This innovative tool provides a centralized location for management and staff to access all the essential information regarding the business's performance.

The beauty of a real estate metrics dashboard lies in its versatility, as it can be configured in various ways based on your specific needs and preferences. Regardless of the configuration, the primary purpose remains the same—to provide you with a comprehensive overview of your business's performance in easily understandable terms.

"Unless commitment is made, there are only promises and hopes; but no plans." —Peter F. Drucker

---

By utilizing the dashboard, both you and your real estate agents will always stay informed about how well you are doing and identify areas for improvement. Similar to the dashboard in your car that provides essential information like speed, gear status, fuel level, or battery charge for electric vehicles, this real estate metrics dashboard empowers you to make informed decisions by tracking daily, quarterly, and annual performance goals.

Some of the key metrics that the dashboard can reveal include the number of visits to your website, the volume of leads generated, the number of contracts closed, the commissions earned, and the actual sales volume compared to the targeted sales. These valuable insights, accumulated over time, allow you to gauge your current performance and shape your future strategies accordingly.

Without this crucial information, it becomes challenging to evaluate your immediate status and project future performance accurately. By regularly monitoring and analyzing these metrics, you and your team can gain a deep understanding of your business's overall performance and identify the indicators of future success.

To stay ahead in the dynamic real estate market, it is essential to research and promptly adapt to any changes that arise. Recent trends have shown increased demand but a dwindling supply, making it even more vital for you to leverage the real estate metrics dashboard to detect market shifts and adjust your strategies accordingly.

"Good business planning is 9 parts execution for every 1 part strategy." —Tim Berry

---

In conclusion, incorporating a real estate metrics dashboard into your business operations will provide you with the essential information needed to make informed decisions, evaluate your performance, and pave the way for future success in the ever-changing real estate landscape.

Dashboard Design and Function

A dashboard provided by specialized software providers offers a convenient way to access crucial information for evaluating your business's performance and KPIs. It puts important data at your fingertips, allowing you to make informed decisions.

To put it into perspective, consider the simplicity of following a football game as an average fan. All you really need to know is the teams playing, the current score, and the time remaining on the clock. Similarly, the metrics displayed on your dashboard can be fully customized to suit the specific needs of your team or brokerage.

Moreover, the dashboard serves as the perfect tool for keeping everyone in your business engaged. With just a quick glance, they can determine whether they are winning or losing in terms of their targets and objectives.

It is crucial, however, to ensure that the dashboard remains simple and user-friendly. As mentioned earlier, it should showcase both leading and lagging indicators of your real estate business. As your business grows, you can continuously adapt and refine the dashboard to align with your evolving needs.

"A business plan is a tool with three basic purposes: communication, management, and planning."
—David Bangs

AROUND THE BLOCK...
INTERVIEW EXCERPTS WITH TOP ECHELON REAL
ESTATE PROFESSIONALS

Carin Nguyen,
The Carin Nguyen Real Estate Network, Phoenix, Arizona

Since I got a coach very early on, there's been an annual plan. I don't know that I really appreciated it and really grabbed onto it though, until I went to Keller Williams and was exposed to it. You could be exposed to the 1-3-5 without Keller Williams, but it wasn't until I went to Keller Williams or started having conversations with them, so I just really appreciate it. And in one of my other coaching organizations, their business plan is super complicated.

From a planning part, it's like, oh okay, I have some of these things so maybe it will be easier to execute, but it does get overwhelming, the lack f simplicity in that plan, so the simplicity of a 1-3-5, and then re-assessing the goals. I'm actually a fan of it. If you're not on track. Let's not just keep at it. If there's a lack of belief and it's getting farther away, you tend to lose your whole group on that, so if you need to do a recalibration, I'm actually a fan of that.

I think one of the things that we've changed in the last six months is not talking about goals. It's like you have a goal. You can set the goal that's up here, but what's the commitment? Let's talk about the floor. Because if you aim high for your goal and you land short, are you actually landing short of what your commitment is? Or your floor? Because if you land under that, you're probably leaving the industry. There's these other variables that take place, and so are you crystal clear on what the floor is? And you need to make sure you're landing between the floor and the goal.

There's the wildly important goal (WIG), and sometimes we get over carried away with the WIG and the BHAG (Big Hairy Audacious Goal), which becomes unattainable not realistic really. And we need to come down to what are we committed to, what is realistic and attainable, and commit to that to be able to then, hey, if we're committed to that, then maybe that stretch goal's going to be attainable and that wig. And maybe it's not.

People have a different belief on realism so I'm actually not even saying realistic. I'm saying what's your must. It's a should or a want versus a must. Your must is going to have your sustainability in the business. That will be the determining factor of whether you're here or not. Because a lot of times, they set the higher goal or the want that should based upon, I should take my family on this Disney cruise, or I should buy this house, or I should do, I should buy an investment property. But those shoulds are more pleasure, and pain is what's going to get you into action, or staying away from pain, I should say. If this pain is, I got to make my house payment and I got to pay my kid's tuition, and I have to, like a must, I will do the things. And then people's financial thermostat tends to be between their must and their wants or should be.

We're at forty agents, and employees, I want to say there are thirteen if we could include the virtual assistants and team leaders, and so on. 2023 is 840 transactions. We want to have a net of seventy-five agents on the team net agents. And I think, what am I missing? I guess volume. It's like 400 million is the number for the volume.

Daniel Beer,
Daniel Beer Home Team CEO & Owner, San Diego, California

I usually start the annual budget or plan in late November or early December, depending on the calendar that year, we do our plan for the following year. That's a two-day offsite. And then quarterly, we have an additional one-day offsite.

We'll have our Q2 offsite. It's probably already on my calendar. If I were to look in my calendar, that date would land somewhere in mid-March. It includes a team and a small group of our most tenured agents. Our 2023 goal is 760 homes sold. It had gross sales of 638 million. Total Team GCI $12.768M

Katharine Loucaidou
Real Estate Group, Bolton, Ontario

I sat through all the business planning and whatever. I've had to come to terms with, I think I don't do it. Because I always feel like if I give myself a plan, I may not get there because of my health or something else.

Everything is floating here. Like I know this year, my goal is this many transactions and I've done it with my team, but for myself, maybe because I've been doing it for so long, I just know where to go. I know how to do it, but I wouldn't like to have the number written down.

Randy Byrd,
Broker, eXp Reality, Santa Rosa, California

I was introduced to an annual plan through coaching. Probably Keller Williams, which was big on that. We were working through the MREA, the Millionaire Real Estate Agent. And we always planned annually with excitement in November and December, but really when I read the book, *The 12 Week Year,* I switched everything up to a ninety-day cycle. And we just plan our annual thought process around a twelve-week cycle because it's more manageable to reach. And then if you don't reach it, it's easy to navigate a course direction change to be able to get to that goal.

So the annual breaks into quarters, but when we think quarters, we think that we still have a lot of football to play. If we think of a football game, well, if you're down twenty to one or twenty to zero in the first quarter, you're like, "We still have three quarters to go." No, you lost the freaking game. You lost twenty to zero. Now, the next game is the next quarter. You've got to beat them in this quarter. And so it's a football analogy, but the honesty of it is, it's an easier goal to hit. It's easier to face, U-turns, and navigation changes to get back on track. And so you can actually reach those annualized goals. That year's over. That's 2022. That's gone.

Now 2023, what are you going to do differently? Do you want to win forty-two to seven or do you want to win twenty-one to zero? What do you want to do?

Bic DeCaro
and Associates, eXp Realty, Ashburn, Virginia

I was introduced to annual plans around 2018 when I got into coaching. Everybody talked about it. I've always had the mindset that there's no way I'm going to fail at something. But it was very much a whirlwind rather than calm and planned out. Because there was no plan, it was just work like crazy and then I would feel burned out.

When I was being coached, I remember just saying to my coach, wow, every year by September! I'm exhausted and I did that little shutdown. And then I'm like, oh shoot, I've got to get back to work again. Then it's like starting over.

So, come January, I was like, ooh, shoot, what do I do now? And how am I going to repeat my amazing year before?

Now we start really early. So by August or September, I'm already starting to plan, and then November's the real critical time.

Now I'm with eXp. So I have two pillars of business. I have my immediate team that I want to grow and then I also have my eXp group that I want to grow. So I'll start with my immediate team. We were going to be on pace to do more than a hundred. But then all the business slowed down toward the end of the year. We just missed it, slightly. We did eight-eight million last year. And our goal now is adjusting it because the market started picking up again. We were doing business plans in November.

I feel now a little bit low because of what was happening in the market. So I said we can just get back up to 1.25 million that would be amazing. And that was just based on November being not so great. Our goal now is 150 million and of course, we'd love to do more. Price has started to increase dramatically over the last six months so it has changed.

I might be shooting low because there's always a ramp-up period to everything, but once you get to a certain point it starts snowballing.

Lindsay Stevens,
eXp Reality, Hudson Valley, New York

No coach had ever done an annual plan with me until Bill Pipes.

Anytime you create a plan, put it in writing. And that comes to life, too. There's accountability behind it. So you know what you have to do. I think the thing, we know, right as leaders and as agents, is that if there is no plan, then the day runs you. You don't run the day. It's the same schedule. I feel like if you asked a hundred agents their excuses or reasons, why they can't do better is that their schedules are not in order. They don't have time. Refining what it is we're trying to accomplish, putting it in writing, and simplifying it. Then, yes, I think you take little bites and then over time, the pebbles lead up to rocks.

Weekly we're going through where we're at to achieve the larger goal. Such as, what step needs to be put in place to achieve what we're trying to achieve this quarter. So, smaller tasks obviously are going to need to happen in order for us to get to the end goal.

I actually just spoke to my team about this. Would they find value in doing similar meetings on an agent level? We're coming up with quarterly rocks and each week we're coming together and they're coming up with their commitments for the week. And where's everybody at?

Because we've done self-directed accountability groups, they're very similar in that they come up with three commitments for the week, one professional and one personal and, you know, we come together every week. Did you hit the commitment? What got in the way in the realm of all the responsibility? Could you have kept the commitment? So it's accountable.

Larry White,
eXp Realty, Houston, Texas

I was introduced to the annual business plan in the real estate industry at an early stage of my career. At my first company, there was a strong focus on the business strategies promoted by influential figures like Mike Ferry, and I would attend events like the Tom Ferry Summit. Each year, we would participate in an annual retreat where we crafted detailed business plans.

Looking back, I realized that this became ingrained in my approach to real estate by my second year in the field. The results spoke for themselves, and as long as I continued to see growth and positive outcomes, I remained dedicated to this practice.

It's important to view real estate as a 90-day cycle, understanding that the actions taken in December, November, and October will impact the success of January. This realization led me to start building our business plan as early as August, allowing us to execute actionable strategies come September. By approaching the year with a well-thought-out plan, we set ourselves up for the potential of experiencing our most successful year yet.